HELPING CHILDREN TO
MANAGE ANGER

Also part of the Helping Children to Build Wellbeing and Resilience series

Helping Children to Manage Transitions
Photocopiable Activity Booklet to Support Wellbeing and Resilience
Deborah M. Plummer
Illustrated by Alice Harper
ISBN 978 1 78775 861 2
eISBN 978 1 78775 862 9

Helping Children to Manage Stress
Photocopiable Activity Booklet to Support Wellbeing and Resilience
Deborah M. Plummer
Illustrated by Alice Harper
ISBN 978 1 78775 865 0
eISBN 978 1 78775 866 7

Using Imagination, Mindful Play and Creative Thinking to Support Wellbeing and Resilience in Children
Deborah M. Plummer
Illustrated by Alice Harper
eISBN 978 1 78775 867 4

Helping Children to Manage Friendships
Photocopiable Activity Booklet to Support Wellbeing and Resilience
Deborah M. Plummer
Illustrated by Alice Harper
ISBN 978 1 78775 868 1
eISBN 978 1 78775 869 8

Helping Children to Build Communication Skills
Photocopiable Activity Booklet to Support Wellbeing and Resilience
Deborah M. Plummer
Illustrated by Alice Harper
ISBN 978 1 78775 870 4
eISBN 978 1 78775 871 1

Helping Children to Build Self-Confidence
Photocopiable Activity Booklet to Support Wellbeing and Resilience
Deborah M. Plummer
Illustrated by Alice Harper
ISBN 978 1 78775 872 8
eISBN 978 1 78775 873 5

Helping Children *to* Manage Anger

Photocopiable Activity Booklet to Support Wellbeing and Resilience

Deborah M. Plummer

Illustrations by Alice Harper

Jessica Kingsley Publishers
London and Philadelphia

Contents

Acknowledgements

I have collected or devised the games and activities in this series of books over a 30-year period of working first as a speech and language therapist with children and adults, and then as a lecturer and workshop facilitator. Some were contributed by children during their participation in therapy groups or by teachers and therapists during workshops and discussions. Thank you!

The suggestions for adaptations and the expansion activities have arisen from my experiences of running children's groups. Many of them combine elements of ImageWork (Dr Dina Glouberman), Personal Construct Theory (see, for example, Peggy Dalton and Gavin Dunnett) and Solution-Focused Brief Therapy (Insoo Kim Berg and Steve de Shazer). My thanks therefore go to my teachers and mentors in these fields.

I have also found the following books helpful:

- Arnold, A. (1976) *The World Book of Children's Games.* London: Pan Books Ltd.
- Beswick, C. (2003) *The Little Book of Parachute Play.* London: Featherstone Education Ltd.
- Brandes, D. and Phillips, H. (1979) *Gamesters' Handbook: 140 Games for Teachers and Group Leaders.* London: Hutchinson.
- Dunn, O. (1978) *Let's Play Asian Children's Games.* Macmillan Southeast Asia in association with the Asian Cultural Centre for UNESCO.
- Liebmann, M. (2004) *Art Therapy for Groups: A Handbook of Themes and Exercises* (2nd edition). London and New York: Routledge.
- Masheder, M. (1989) *Let's Play Together.* London: Green Print.
- Neelands, J. (1990) *Structuring Drama Work: A Handbook of Available Forms in Theatre and Drama.* Cambridge: Cambridge University Press.

Note: There are many different non-competitive 'mini' games that can be used for choosing groups, coordinators (leaders) and order of play where appropriate. I have listed several options in the

accompanying eBook Using Imagination, Mindful Play and Creative Thinking to Support Wellbeing and Resilience in Children. *I suggest that the format is varied between sessions so that children can experiment with different ways of doing this. The choosing then becomes part of the personal learning.*

The following icons are used throughout to indicate the three elements of the IMPACT approach:

Imagination

Mindful Play

Creative Thinking

Introduction

This book is one of a series based on the use of Imagination (I), Mindful Play (MP) and Creative Thinking (CT) to enhance social, psychological and emotional wellbeing and resilience in children. IMPACT activities and strategies encourage children to build life skills through carefully structured and supportive play experiences. Emphasis is given to the important role played by adult facilitators in creating a safe space in which children can share and explore feelings and difficulties and experiment with different ways of thinking and 'being'. This approach is explained in the accompanying eBook *Using Imagination, Mindful Play and Creative Thinking to Support Wellbeing and Resilience in Children*, which also contains many further ideas for games and activities and examples of how the IMPACT approach can enhance daily interactions with children.

Please remember, if you are a parent or carer and you are concerned about ongoing and persistently high levels of anxiety or aggressive behaviour or persistently low mood in your child, it is always best to seek further support via your child's school or your child's doctor. This book is not intended as a substitute for the professional help that may be needed.

USING THIS BOOK

The games and activities in this book help children to:

- understand that anger is a normal, healthy emotion
- identify some of their worries and concerns about managing strong emotions
- identify their current strengths and skills
- develop or consolidate specific skills and strategies that will be useful for managing angry feelings

- explore the possible benefits and enjoyment that can result from having some control over how they express their feelings.

The IMPACT approach emphasizes eight *foundation elements* for wellbeing (see the accompanying eBook *Using Imagination, Mindful Play and Creative Thinking to Support Wellbeing and Resilience in Children*). All eight of these elements are closely interconnected and each will have relevance for children who are learning to manage angry feelings. The focus for the games and activities in this book centres on two of the elements that are of particular significance in exploring anger: *self-awareness* and *self and others*. Here is a reminder of what these two foundation elements encapsulate:

Self-awareness
Self-awareness is the cornerstone of realistic self-evaluation. It involves:

- developing the ability to be focused in the here and now rather than being absorbed in unhelpful thoughts about the past or future – this includes awareness and identification of feelings as they arise
- developing the ability to switch attention appropriately from external events to internal thoughts and feelings and vice versa
- understanding that emotional, mental and physical changes are a natural part of life
- being aware of the normality of a range of feelings and how these link to thoughts and behaviour.

The IMPACT approach offers a forum in which feelings are acknowledged, valued and openly discussed in a non-judgemental way. The games and activities help children to develop the ability to switch attention effectively between internal and external stimuli, cope more effectively with distractions, make informed choices about how and when to focus their attention, monitor their internal 'self-talk' and build effective strategies for emotion regulation.

Self and others
One of the most important aspects of wellbeing is our connection with others. Helping children to negotiate friendships is also central to helping them to build resilience.

Self and others involves:

- understanding the joys and challenges of relationships: learning to trust and

9

to negotiate and cooperate with others; being able to see things from another person's perspective (empathy); learning respect and tolerance for other people's needs and views

- developing and maintaining personal identity while still recognizing the natural mutuality and *inter*dependence of relationships
- recognizing other people's emotions, distinguishing personal feelings from those of others
- developing a sense of family/cultural 'stories'
- understanding *universal* values and guiding principles.

IMPACT activities explore aspects of group cooperation and trust, and aim to promote an understanding of how our thoughts and actions affect our relationships with other people. They aim to help children to identify with appropriate role models and to encourage the ability to work with or alongside other children and adults with awareness, tolerance and empathy. Engagement in shared attention activities also helps children to direct their focus and concentration without being inappropriately distracted by others.

Facilitator involvement

All the games and activities in this series of books offer opportunities for facilitators to take an active part. Our participation reflects the nature of extended communities and gives us an opportunity to have fun alongside the children. Throughout the games in this book, the term 'game coordinator' therefore refers to either adult or child participants, as appropriate for the level and stage of each group.

Activities

The first section of games and activities, 'IMPACT Essentials for Managing Anger' (section II), introduces children to the central features of the IMPACT approach – using imagery, being mindful and thinking creatively. There are also games and activities for group 'gelling' and for exploring relevant concepts such as self-respect and respect for others. Each book in this series has a different set of IMPACT essentials. With a slight change of emphasis, you will be able to use any of these to supplement your sessions if needed.

The remainder of the sections are arranged in accordance with specific aspects of managing anger: 'Working Together', 'Exploring Emotions and Degrees of Emotion', 'Exploring Strategies for Emotion Regulation', 'Causes and Consequences' and 'Recognizing Achievements and Celebrating'. You might also find it useful to add a selection of activities from *Helping Children to Manage Stress* and *Helping Children to Manage Friendships*, which are available in this series.

The creative potential for supporting skill development is one of the wonderful features of childhood games. I have given several suggestions for specific skills that might be learned or further developed during each game and its associated activities, but these are not exhaustive. You may want to add more to suit your own focus of work.

Ideas are also suggested for adaptations. (See also Chapter 12, 'Adapting Activities', in the accompanying eBook *Using Imagination, Mindful Play and Creative Thinking to Support Wellbeing and Resilience in Children*.) These illustrate some of the many ways in which a basic game or activity can be simplified or made more complex to suit diverse developmental levels, strengths and learning differences.

I suggest that you close each session with a round of appreciation, a focused breathing exercise (see *Using Imagination, Mindful Play and Creative Thinking to Support Wellbeing and Resilience in Children*) or a sharing of insights. For example:

Today I found out that...

Today I really liked the game of...

I'm feeling...

I appreciate...

Reflection and discussion

Another important aspect of all the games and activities is the opportunity they provide for children to expand their creative and critical thinking skills. To aid this process, I have included suggestions for further reflection and discussion ('Talk about'). These include a mixture of possible prompt questions and suggestions for comments or explanations that can be useful when introducing or elaborating some of the ideas. (See Chapter 11, 'Mindful Communication', and Chapter 13, 'Mindful Praise and Appreciation', in *Using Imagination, Mindful Play and Creative Thinking to Support Wellbeing and Resilience in Children* for more ideas about facilitating discussions with children.) You may want to select just a couple of these or spread the discussion over several sessions.

These discussion topics also provide an opportunity for drawing links between different themes at later times. You could remind children of particular games or activities when this is relevant: 'Do you remember when we played that game of... What did you find out about listening?' or 'How might the skills we needed for the consequence game be useful to us in this situation?'

Expansion activities

Most of the games in this book are followed by one or more expansion activities and/ or are directly linked with a second game (which could be used in the same session or at a later time). These expansion activities and linked games are an important part of the process. They encourage children to recognize the benefits of a stepped approach to learning and to the process of change, understand how new skills can build on previous experiences, and understand how current skills can be strengthened.

Activity sheets

Some of the expansion activities have accompanying activity sheets that can also be adapted for discussion, these can be found in section VIII. I have found that children particularly like to draw or write about their imaginary world. Their drawings and jottings might then be the starting point for wellbeing stories (see the accompanying eBook *Using Imagination, Mindful Play and Creative Thinking to Support Wellbeing and Resilience in Children* for ideas about how to create these stories). They can also be made into a personal 'Book of Wisdom' and perhaps act as reminders of some of the strategies that children might want to use again in the future.

Note: Please keep in mind that IMPACT activity sheets are offered as supplementary material to expand and reinforce each child's learning experiences. They are not intended as stand-alone alternatives to the mindful play and supportive discussions that are central to the IMPACT approach.

Exploring Anger

Imagine the following scene:

Brenda is preparing to walk with her three-year-old son Ryan and her daughter Hayley (age seven) to Hayley's school. They normally go by car, but today they have to get the bus. They are running late because Hayley can't find her shoes. Brenda dresses Ryan while calling out instructions to Hayley. They set off to the bus stop. Hayley is chatting to her mum about school, but Brenda is preoccupied with Ryan who doesn't want to hold her hand and keeps pulling away from her. They walk past the park and Ryan sees the swings. He suddenly screeches 'No!' and sits down on the pavement, kicking his legs furiously. He manages to kick his mum as she tries to pick him up. Brenda shouts at Ryan. Hayley starts to cry and throws down her book bag with such force that her reading book falls out and lands in a puddle.

It is conceivable that Hayley might have a pretty miserable start to her school day! Ryan may quickly forget his frustration if he is distracted and reassured, but his sister is old enough to brood on the various events of the morning. Her thoughts may fuel anxiety ('Will I get into trouble because of the reading book?' 'Will I be late for school?') and feelings of annoyance ('It's Ryan's fault, he gets all the attention'). These mixed emotions may in turn affect her concentration and performance in the classroom, and may even lead to an uncharacteristic display of annoyance toward another child. In this instance Brenda retrieves the situation with a bit of expert mothering. She hugs Ryan, acknowledges that he is 'a bit cross' and distracts his attention from the swings. She simultaneously cuddles Hayley, apologizes for not paying attention to her, rescues the book, acknowledges Hayley's feelings of anxiety, reassures her, and still manages to get everyone to the bus stop on time!

The different degrees of annoyance, anxiety and frustration felt by Hayley, Ryan and Brenda are all normal responses to an accumulation of events. Strategies were put into place quickly and Ryan and Hayley learned the value of self-calming through their mother's support and model. Such common scenarios illustrate several points that are relevant to understanding childhood anger:

- Young children need help in learning how to manage their feelings.
- Anger can be experienced and expressed in different ways and to differing degrees. It is helpful for children to know and be able to use a range of feeling words that reflect different intensities.
- Children need to know that they can feel angry and still be loved. It is helpful if adults show that they can cope with a child's angry feelings in a calm way.
- Most anger occurs in the context of a trigger event or is secondary to another underlying emotion.
- Managing angry feelings successfully may involve modelling and teaching a number of different skills and strategies.

YOUNG CHILDREN NEED HELP IN LEARNING HOW TO MANAGE THEIR FEELINGS

For many of us, 'childhood anger' conjures up images of aggression and of children who are 'out of control' or 'troubled'. But anger in itself is not necessarily an unwelcome emotion. In fact, it can sometimes be a force for positive change. When it is expressed appropriately and meaningfully it can be a perfectly normal and healthy response to injustice, for example, and can act as an energizer and a motivator for action. Anger is also a basic survival response that enables us to react instantly to threatening situations and to defend ourselves in times of crisis. However, repeated bouts of childhood anger can lead to feelings of confusion and can be a frightening experience for children.

Neuro nugget

There is now considerable research that links low levels of the 'feel-good' hormone serotonin with aggressive behaviour. Serotonin has many functions, including affecting certain areas of the prefrontal cortex that are involved in controlling and inhibiting aggression and anger. When we are under attack and need to defend ourselves, the body reduces the production of serotonin and produces high levels of norepinephrine. This hormone, also known as noradrenaline, plays an important part in preparing the body for action in an emergency. In irritable aggression, on the other hand, both serotonin *and* norepinephrine are reduced.[1]

The challenge for adults is to help all children to develop the key skills and capacities for emotion regulation, a task that starts in babyhood and continues throughout the early years as children watch and monitor their primary caregivers and then begin to interact with the wider world. The ability to regulate our emotions is an important factor in healthy self-esteem and in the ability to form and sustain successful relationships with others. It involves recognizing different emotions in ourselves and in others, understanding the nature of these emotions and what signals they are giving us ('What am I feeling?' 'How will I respond?'), and learning to manage intense emotions in a healthy and effective way so that they do not overwhelm us.

Margot Sunderland highlights the importance of helping children to manage intense feelings in order to minimize the negative effects of stress when they are older:

> When a child is not helped enough with his intense feelings, the alarm systems in his lower brain can be over-active in later life. This means that he may over-react to minor stressors, 'sweat the small stuff', and live a life of worrying, and/or be angry or short-tempered for much of the time.[2]

Children who experience intense anger will often look to adults to give them a sense of containment and safety. If this need is not met, they may become more and more anxious, and their angry behaviour may increase in their attempt to gain attention and recognition of their distress. In addition, inappropriate expressions of anger are likely to engender negative responses from peers. Classmates will tend to avoid persistently angry children, and this can lead to further anxiety and feelings associated with low self-esteem.

1   Gerhardt, S. (2015) *Why Love Matters: How Affection Shapes a Baby's Brain* (2nd edition). London and New York: Routledge.
2   Sunderland, M. (2006) *The Science of Parenting*. London: Dorling Kindersley, p.27. [There is a second edition of this book, published in 2016.]

ANGER CAN BE EXPERIENCED AND EXPRESSED IN DIFFERENT WAYS AND TO DIFFERING DEGREES

The ways in which children experience feelings of anger and the ways in which they express these feelings are partly determined by their developmental level and partly reinforced by the reactions of others and by family patterns and past experiences.

Informal observations of children at play will quickly reveal that whereas some youngsters are more prone to direct expression of anger either verbally or physically, others are more likely to suppress their anger or to express it indirectly (for example, through withdrawal into passive silence or through tears). Sometimes this suppression is a learned response due to the disapproval of caregivers or to experiences of being rejected when anger is shown. Constant repression or denial of anger can be detrimental to a child's emotional and physical wellbeing too. It may, for example, lead to depression in later life, and has also been linked with lowered immunity due to the ongoing release of stress hormones, particularly cortisol, in the body.[3]

The word 'anger' is also often used to cover a whole range of emotional intensity including mild irritation or frustration, so it is something that we are likely to come across in others, or to experience in ourselves, on a fairly regular basis. If we handle it successfully then we can help children to understand that anger need not be a frightening, unpredictable or overwhelming experience, and that they do have the capacity to cope with this emotion in a productive and healthy manner. It is therefore also helpful for children to be able to recognize a range of emotions and to develop the vocabulary to name and describe them.[4]

CHILDREN NEED TO KNOW THAT THEY CAN FEEL ANGRY AND STILL BE LOVED

If angry feelings are frightening for a child, it will be helpful for them to see that adults are not fazed by strong emotions and that we will not ignore their need for attention. When we show that we understand why a child might be feeling angry, and we focus on the child's thoughts and actions, we are able to show them that feelings of anger

---

3   Gerhardt, S. (2015) *Why Love Matters: How Affection Shapes a Baby's Brain* (2nd edition). London and New York: Routledge.

4   Some psychologists make a distinction between feelings (such as feelings of wellbeing, thirst or pain) and emotions (such as anger or sadness). Since we don't tend to do this in our daily interactions, I have used the terms interchangeably in the relevant games and activities.

don't make them a 'bad' person. This also opens the way for them to learn and to use appropriate strategies.

The mindful aspects of IMPACT games and activities will minimize the possibility of angry outbursts happening during a small group session, but it is always useful to have a strategy in mind and to share this with others so that children experience consistency in the ways that adults respond to displays of anger. The following three-step support strategy can be helpful in these circumstances.

1. Clarify

It is important to make a distinction between the child's feeling of anger and any unacceptable or inappropriate behaviour. Give a clear message about the behaviour first: 'No. We do not accept spitting in this classroom'; 'No. It is not okay to swear at me when you are angry.' Keep your voice calm, but firm.

2. Acknowledge

Acknowledge the child's distress. It may seem obvious to say 'I can see you're angry' but this confirms that you have noted their distress and that you take it seriously. It also provides an opportunity to reflect back to them a different degree of emotion that might be more appropriate. For example, 'I can see you're angry. I'd be *fed up* too if that happened to me.'

3. Time out

When a child feels flooded with emotion, reasoned discussion is probably not an option as they are unlikely to be able to think logically or take on board what is being said. Offering them 'time out' to allow the body to calm down is usually necessary. It is important to structure this carefully, otherwise, rather than giving them time to cool down, 'time out' can actually fuel the anger. As Goleman points out: 'a cooling-down period will not work if that time is used to pursue the train of anger-inducing thought, since each such thought is in itself a minor trigger for more cascades of anger.'[5]

If the objective is to give the child a chance to become calmer before entering into a rational discussion or before clearing up any damage or apologizing for hurting someone, then the time might be more productively spent employing a specific self-calming strategy – one that they could possibly use in the future before things get out of hand (see section V).

5   Goleman, D. (1996) *Emotional Intelligence: Why It Can Matter More than IQ*. London: Bloomsbury, p.63. [There is a new 2020 edition of this book, also published by Bloomsbury.]

MOST ANGER OCCURS IN THE CONTEXT OF A TRIGGER EVENT OR IS SECONDARY TO ANOTHER UNDERLYING EMOTION

Most instances of childhood anger can be traced to a 'trigger' event or an underlying emotion such as frustration, sadness, fear or anxiety. These triggers are often masked or overshadowed by the actual displays of anger in young children – the original source of a child's angry feelings may go unrecognized, with more emphasis being made of the perception that they have 'trouble with anger'. The child may not even recognize the original trigger and may be unable to explain why they hit out or lost their temper with a friend. In helping children to manage angry feelings it is always helpful to be aware of the contexts in which these feelings might have been generated and to help children to understand these connections. Some of the most common triggers are outlined below.

Self-esteem

The link between self-esteem and aggressive behaviour has long been recognized. Healthy levels of self-esteem allow a child to cope with many of life's difficulties without feeling 'got at' or victimized. However, when self-esteem is low, the threshold for anger may also be low and an angry response can be triggered much more easily. Children who have specific behavioural difficulties may also seek out opportunities to confirm their feelings of low self-worth by entering into conflict with others or by behaving in a way that invites rejection.[6]

Stress

There are many aspects of daily life that young children find physically, emotionally or mentally stressful for short periods of time. Small amounts of positive stress are normal and help a child to feel motivated to achieve. But where stress is excessive or continuous over a long period of time, even at relatively low levels, they will experience a 'toxic' build-up of stress hormones such as cortisol, and angry feelings will be engendered much more easily (see *Helping Children to Manage Stress*, which is available in this series).

Continuous stress of this sort may, for example, be due to ongoing bullying, anxiety about a parent who has a chronic illness, uncertainty or unpredictability at home or pressure to achieve beyond a child's capabilities. Persistent under-stimulation (boredom) can also register in the brain as stress. Whereas adults are able to do something

---

6   Booker, O. (1999) *Averting Aggression: Safe Work in Services for Adolescents and Young Adults* (2nd edition). Lyme Regis: Russell House Publishing.

to relieve boredom, young children have fewer choices about how to do this and may resort to temper tantrums or fighting.

Another, often misunderstood, area of stress is related to speech, language and communication delay or disorder. While many children seem to cope with speech or language impairment with remarkable fortitude, there are some who become acutely troubled by feelings of anger rooted in the inherent frustrations of their communication difficulty. For example, many children who stammer have difficulty in negotiating with others and in verbally 'standing up' for themselves when they have been unfairly accused, or their talents and successes go unrecognized. Children with language impairments often do not have the vocabulary to label or describe complex emotions or the internal language capacity (self-talk) to help themselves to regulate their emotions.

Insecurity

The link between primary caregiver and child attachment patterns and the child's later ability to self-regulate has been the focus for much research. For example, an early relationship that is harsh or punitive may result in an insecure avoidant attachment where the child avoids contact with their primary caregiver, rather than seeking contact, when they are anxious. Children experiencing this type of relationship are much more likely to be aggressive when they are older.[7]

Similarly, uncertainty in the constancy of the primary caregiver can continue to manifest itself later in childhood as anger directed against other adults, including teachers. These children often want support and attention, but at the same time become anxious in the presence of adults, an ambiguous state that can result in anger when a caring adult tries to help.

Sadness

Profound sadness, for example due to the loss of a family member, can make a child more vulnerable to bouts of unexplained anger as they try to cope with feelings of abandonment and uncertainty. Extensive research with adolescents suffering from periods of depression shows a strong correlation between feelings of deep sadness and feelings of anger.[8] This research also offers insights into how younger children often experience a blend of these two emotions.

---

7   Gerhardt, S. (2015) *Why Love Matters: How Affection Shapes a Baby's Brain* (2nd edition). London and New York: Routledge.

8   Harter, S. (1999) *The Construction of the Self*. New York: Guilford Press.

Frustration

I have already mentioned frustration in connection with communication difficulties, but of course frustration is also an inevitable part of many other developmental hurdles that all children learn to negotiate. Youngsters will have countless experiences of feeling frustrated when they cannot have something or cannot do something because they are too little, too young or don't yet have the necessary knowledge or dexterity. Older children may experience frustration when something they have spent a long time over is spoiled accidentally or their hard work is not acknowledged. Children who have a tendency towards 'perfectionism' can easily become frustrated and destroy their own work when they make a small mistake.

While most children learn to tolerate a certain amount of frustration as they get older, when such feelings are frequent or the child has not developed a healthy degree of emotional resilience, then either self-directed anger or anger towards others is a likely consequence. These children often find it hard to ask for help with a task before frustration sets in – asking for assistance may be closely linked with fear of (or confirmation of) failure, thus compounding feelings of low self-worth. In these circumstances telling a child that it is 'okay to ask' may not be sufficient to help them to get over this hurdle.

Other, more immediate, triggers to anger include:

- jealousy and sibling rivalry
- a sense of being treated unfairly, such as being punished for something that they didn't do
- embarrassment
- disappointment
- an adult intervening to 'help out' when this was not needed
- seeing injustice done to others
- humiliation
- loss of control/sense of autonomy
- lack of understanding by others (empathy)
- lack of the child's ability to empathize with others
- others denying or rejecting the child's genuine feelings
- hunger
- tiredness
- illness/pain.

MANAGING ANGRY FEELINGS SUCCESSFULLY MAY INVOLVE MODELLING AND TEACHING A NUMBER OF DIFFERENT SKILLS AND STRATEGIES

It is helpful for children to be able to try a number of different strategies and to further develop appropriate skills. For example, Sue Gerhardt refers to three strategies that young children might use in naturally controlling angry impulses: the ability to self-distract, the ability to seek information about the obstacles to the desired goals and the use of comfort-seeking strategies:

> One study found that 3-year-olds who were skilled in using all three strategies showed the least aggressive and externalizing behaviour (Gilliom *et al.* 2002).[9] They were able to control themselves sufficiently to turn away from the source of frustration and focus on something else, and were less likely to attack it. They could also ask questions about when the situation would be alleviated, which was very helpful in dissolving anger.[10]

A MINDFUL PLAY PERSPECTIVE

We want each child to know and understand that they are much more than their angry feelings. We also want to help them to identify their existing skills and strengths and to feel more in control of their emotional, mental and physical responses to difficult situations. However, talking about strong emotions and focusing on controlling and redirecting emotional energy can be an exhausting process for children and, if over-done, could be counter-productive. For these reasons the emphasis for the games and activities in this book goes beyond strategies that children can use to calm their anger. The IMPACT approach gives weight to building skills of focusing, cooperation and negotiation, promoting feelings of self-efficacy and self-control, understanding empathy and learning to tolerate frustration. Children are invited to experiment and problem-solve, to arrive at their own conclusions and ultimately to experience a different sense of wellbeing where anger is not the dominant theme.

9   Gilliom, M., Shaw, D., Beck, J., Schonberg, M. and Lukon, J. (2002) 'Anger regulation in disadvantaged pre-school boys.' *Developmental Psychology 38*, 2, 222.

10   Gerhardt, S. (2015) *Why Love Matters: How Affection Shapes a Baby's Brain* (2nd edition). London and New York: Routledge, pp.207–208.

With these foundations in place children will then be more able to channel justified anger into appropriate responses and to recognize and defuse inappropriate manifestations of this emotion.

The IMPACT approach also offers ways for adults to develop or increase their ability to feel comfortable with children's anger and to reflect on their interactions with children. It is helpful if as many key adults as possible know which strategies and goals a child is working towards. These can then be noticed and encouraged as appropriate (see Chapter 13, 'Mindful Praise and Appreciation', in the accompanying eBook *Using Imagination, Mindful Play and Creative Thinking to Support Wellbeing and Resilience in Children*). When adults and peers acknowledge a child's skills and abilities in a variety of situations, this can be a key factor in building their self-esteem and maintaining motivation. You might also be in a position to initiate a whole class or whole school strategy for managing anger, and this would be ideal in helping children to see that this is a normal emotion and that everyone benefits from learning ways of understanding anger and working with it.

In order to get a feel for the ways in which the IMPACT approach works in regard to managing anger, I invite you to 'play' with the remaining exploratory activities in this section. There are no 'right' or 'wrong' answers; they are just ways of exploring the topic.

Begin by setting aside a short period of uninterrupted time when you will have the opportunity to carry out and to reflect on a single activity – 10–15 minutes is probably ample. I suggest that you only do one activity and then go back to doing other things. Please don't be tempted to do all the activities one after the other in a single sitting, even if you have the time. A period of reflection is always useful after an exploratory activity.

Exploratory activity 1.1. First thoughts

Ask yourself:

- What, if anything, might worry me about a child's anger?
- How might an angry outburst from a child affect how I feel and act?
- What degrees of anger do I recognize in myself?
- How do I normally express feelings of anger?
- What are my strengths with regard to helping children to regulate their emotions?

Exploratory activity 1.2. Triggers to anger
(See the activities in section VI.)

- Make a list of five situations that you know might trigger a *feeling* of frustration or anger for you and five situations that you think a particular child would find frustrating or embarrassing and which might trigger *displays* of anger in them. Note some of the similarities and differences.
- Make a note of your personal anger management strategies. On a scale of 1–5, where 1 is slightly successful and 5 is very successful, how successful do you feel your current strategies are?

Exploratory activity 1.3. Focusing
(See activities '6. Fruit salad' and '7. All birds fly'.)

For this activity you will need to be seated in a comfortable upright position. You may want to close your eyes to help you to focus your attention.

Take a few moments to focus on different areas of your body and notice whatever sensation is there. Start with your left foot and then allow the focus of your attention to very gradually move along the left side of your body and along your left arm into your hand. What sensations do you notice? For example, are your feet warm, cold, tingling? Just notice whatever sensations are there without trying to change anything. If other thoughts come to mind you will be able to notice them and then let them go, bringing your awareness back to your body. Now move your attention to your right foot, your right leg, your right arm and hand. Then notice your neck, jaw and forehead. Sit for a few moments sensing your whole body. When you are ready, open your eyes. Sketch a body outline of yourself and jot down anything that you noticed and where.

There are many different ways in which children can learn to enhance their abilities to focus attention and this is explored more fully in the accompanying eBook *Using Imagination, Mindful Play and Creative Thinking to Support Wellbeing and Resilience in Children*. With regard to managing feelings of anger, focusing on body sensations can be particularly useful for children as it can help them to recognize the early signs of rising anger (the physical signs of the fight or flight response).

USING IMAGERY

(See Chapter 8, 'Imagination and Images', and Chapter 9, 'Image-Making', in *Using Imagination, Mindful Play and Creative Thinking to Support Wellbeing and Resilience in Children* and, for example, '8. Imagining', '23. Shaping up!' and '24. In the hot seat' in this book.)

Exploratory activity 1.4. Finding an image

Take a moment to settle yourself in a comfortable position. Become aware of the sensation of your body in the chair. Simply notice how your body feels. Gradually take your attention to your breathing. Allow your natural breathing to become the focus of your attention, feeling the flow of air in and out of your body. When you are ready, allow this focus to fade and then allow an image to come to mind that somehow represents how you are feeling right now. It might be an object, a plant, an animal or a colour – just allow the image to 'emerge'. When you are ready, briefly sketch or write about this image. There is no need to think about this too deeply. You may find that you want to add to or change your image in some way at a later point.

Constructive use of the imagination is central to the IMPACT approach. Images have a remarkable capacity to sum up how we are feeling or how we view a situation. So, for example, I have just tuned into my own image of how I am feeling. What emerged was a cotton reel. I was momentarily concerned that there wasn't much cotton left on the reel, but when I took the perspective of the reel I realized that this felt okay – I have been stitching together a lot of different aspects of my work and the project is nearly completed. I could follow this metaphor in all sorts of directions, but then I would be using my rational mind too much – this type of image represents a moment in time, it doesn't need to be analysed, but it can offer useful insights.

A STEPPED APPROACH

Sometimes changes in the ways children handle difficult situations are very small and gradual and this is not always easy for them to accept. Helping a child to understand a stepped approach to change and knowing how current skills can be used, and new skills can be learned, can help them to maintain motivation.

Exploratory activity 1.5. Pyramiding

This is based on an exercise from Personal Construct Theory.[11] Because it is such a useful tool, I have included different versions of this in some of the other books in this series too.

Think of a word or phrase that represents your personal view of the opposite of 'uncontrolled anger'. Now think of a child whom you consider is generally in this positive mental, emotional and physical state. Let's say your personal opposite to 'uncontrollable anger' is 'emotional balance'. At the top of a large sheet of paper write down four attributes or skills that this child has that cause you to view them as 'able to achieve emotional balance'. You could start off by thinking 'I know this because...'

Now take each of these four attributes or skills in turn and ask yourself *how* you know this. How does this child demonstrate each attribute or skill? How would other people know this about them? For example, if one of your observations is 'able to self-calm', think about how that can be broken down into smaller components. What does the ability to self-calm 'look' like? Do this for as many of your ideas as possible so that you are refining them into smaller and smaller constituents.

Whenever you find yourself using a word or phrase that denotes a negative, such as 'not', 'never' or 'doesn't', look for a positive alternative. For example, if 'self-calming' includes 'doesn't get physically tense', you might change this to 'able to let go of unnecessary tension'. You could then further refine this by asking yourself 'what does this child do, or what sort of language do they use, that conveys to others that they can let go of unnecessary tension?'

11   See, for example, Dalton, P. and Dunnett, G. (2005) *A Psychology for Living: Personal Construct Theory for Professionals and Clients* (2nd edition). Chichester: John Wiley & Sons Ltd.

When you have at least ten concrete examples of how this child demonstrates that they are able to achieve emotional balance, bring to mind a second child who needs help with this ability. Is there anything in your list that this second child is already doing? This will be your starting point. However small, there is always something that can be highlighted as evidence of a change already happening.

Knowing some of the theory behind anger management strategies is important. It helps us to be reflective and creative in our support. But, of course, this is only part of the picture. When we are mindful of our role and of the feelings and experiences of the children in our care, when we value imagination as a powerful tool for change, and when we can impart a sense of fun into exploring such complex emotions as anger, we are well on the way to helping children build the emotional balance and resilience that is so vital for their wellbeing.

SUGGESTIONS FOR FURTHER READING

Geddes, H. (2006) *Attachment in the Classroom: The Links Between Children's Early Experience, Emotional Well-Being and Performance in School.* London: Worth Publishing Ltd.

Gulbenkoglu, H. and Hagiliassis, N. (2006) *Anger Management: An Anger Management Training Package for Individuals with Disabilities.* London and Philadelphia, PA: Jessica Kingsley Publishers.

Stringer, B. and Mall, M. (1999) *A Solution Focused Approach to Anger Management with Children.* Birmingham: The Questions Publishing Company Ltd and Birmingham LEA.

IMPACT Essentials for Managing Anger

By doing the activities in this section you will be helping children to:

- think about different aspects of themselves, not just how they are dealing with any current difficulties
- identify their strengths and skills
- begin to explore how the ability to imagine can be a helpful resource
- develop or consolidate their skills in focusing and attending.

1. Important names

Wellbeing focus:

☑ Self-awareness   ☑ Self and others

Examples of personal skills learned or consolidated:

☑ Listening   ☑ Taking turns
☑ Self-control   ☑ Focusing attention
☑ Speaking in a group

Examples of general/social learning:

☑ Developing self-respect and   ☑ Building group cohesion
   respect for others

This is a useful introductory game, particularly for a new group, but it could also be played in a group where everyone already knows each other. The emphasis is on self-respect and respect for others, which is explored further in the next activity, '2. Magic threes'.

How to play

Each child chooses a special word to describe themselves, beginning with the first letter of their name (for example, 'energetic Erin', 'happy Hilary'). Players stand in a circle and use a soft ball or beanbag to throw. On the first round the catcher says their own special name. On the second round the thrower calls out another child's special name as they throw the soft ball or beanbag to them. (See more ideas for adapting soft ball and beanbag games in the accompanying eBook *Using Imagination, Mindful Play and Creative Thinking to Support Wellbeing and Resilience in Children*.)

Adaptations

- The children choose special names to reflect their talents or enthusiasms, such as 'Demon Dancer Jack' or 'Maths Magician Sarah'.
- Use a bell to add a sense of grandeur to the sound of each name. The first

player carries the bell slowly across the circle to another child, trying not to let it ring. This also encourages physical self-control. The child who receives the bell rings it once and says their special name as the chime resonates around the room (younger children can just say their first name). They then carry the bell across the circle to another child and so on, until everyone has had a turn.

Talk about

Think about the enjoyment of saying and hearing your own name. How can you celebrate your name? Take time to reflect on the qualities in yourself that you really like. Why is self-respect important? How do we show self-respect? How do we show respect for others?

EXPANSION ACTIVITY 1.1. MARK OF RESPECT

Players make and decorate their own name badge. Instead of writing their names they could choose to draw, paint or use any available craft materials to make a badge that somehow represents an aspect of their personality, one that they particularly value. This need not be explained to others. Players wear their badge of self-respect for the session. These should be treated with care when the session has ended. They might want to give them to you for safekeeping or put them in a folder with any other artwork or activity sheets that they complete during your time together. Talk with them about the importance of respecting their own creative pieces of work.

2. Magic threes

Wellbeing focus:

☑ Self-awareness ☑ Self and others

Examples of personal skills learned or consolidated:

☑ Focusing attention ☑ Taking turns
☑ Concentration ☑ Listening
☑ Memory strategies

Examples of general/social learning:

☑ Developing self-respect and respect for others ☑ Building trust
☑ Building group cohesion
☑ Appreciating diversity

This game and the expansion activity continue to reinforce concepts of self-respect and respect for others (see '1. Important names'). Children can see that they are appreciated members of the group just for being themselves.

How to play
Players have three minutes to walk around the room and introduce themselves to three other people. Each child tells these three people three important facts about themselves. For younger children this could be their name or nickname, something they hate and something they like. For older children it might be their greatest achievement, their best birthday and their most treasured possession, or one thing that makes them cross, one thing they do to 'chill out' and one thing they want to achieve.

When the time is up, everyone sits in a circle and recounts as much information about as many other children as possible.

Adaptations

- Pairs share the information and then introduce each other to the rest of the group.

- Players divide into groups of three or four and try to find three things that they all have in common. One person from each small group tells the whole group what these three things are.

Talk about

How difficult or easy was it to remember what you heard? What would make it easier/harder to remember facts about other people? Why is it important to remember what people tell us about themselves? What does it feel like when someone remembers something important about you? What does it feel like when people get the facts wrong?

How can a memory game like this help you with other tasks and skills (for example, remembering strategies for self-calming)?

What does this game tell us about respecting ourselves and others?

What does it feel like to know that you have things in common with other people? Was it difficult or easy to find things in common?

EXPANSION ACTIVITY 2.1. SUPERPOWER SHIELD

Each child draws a shield that has pictures or words to show three important facts about who they are and what they enjoy doing – what three things is it really important for other people to know about them? These things give them 'superpowers' for wellbeing. Display the shields on a wall for everyone to admire.

3. Sort us out

Wellbeing focus:

- ☑ Self-awareness
- ☑ Self and others

Examples of personal skills learned or consolidated:

- ☑ Observation
- ☑ Listening
- ☑ Organizing
- ☑ Cooperation
- ☑ Sequencing

Examples of general/social learning:

- ☑ Being part of a group
- ☑ Understanding rules made by other people
- ☑ Understanding diversity
- ☑ Understanding concept of peer pressure

This game gives children the opportunity to think about ways in which both similarities and differences between individuals can strengthen group cohesion and effectiveness.

This game is paired with '28. Sorted!' It is useful for children to see how the same game or activity can be used in many different ways. You could introduce this concept by asking the group to be inventive in how they might adapt this activity, to explore degrees of emotion or to decide a sequence of events for making a kite or baking a cake, for example.

How to play
The game coordinator times the group while they arrange themselves in a line according to one or more of the following criteria:

- alphabetically, according to the first letter of their first name
- according to house number
- according to age
- according to what time they get up in the morning.

Adaptations

- The children choose their own criteria for organizing the group into a line.
- Smaller groups of children stand on a PE bench and then try to arrange themselves according to different criteria without stepping off the bench.
- The game is played with criteria chosen that do not need any verbal interaction (for example, height, groups of children with the same eye colour or hair colour).

Talk about

Which line took the least time to organize? Why was this? Which grouping took the longest? Why do you think this was? For each grouping everyone had at least one thing in common, but within the grouping there were differences. What might happen if we all looked exactly the same or we all had the same name? What might be good about all being the same?

Think about similarities and differences and how you could be members of several different groups such as family groups, friendship groups, sports groups or school groups. How does it feel to be a member of a particular group of friends? What is it like to be part of more than one group? What are some of the good things about being in more than one group? When is it not so helpful to have separate groupings?

What are the rules for this game? What are some of the rules that help to make a game feel safe? (See also '21. Waves on the sea parachute game', and the 'Talk about' section, for this.)

Sometimes rules are 'unspoken'. How do you find out about the different rules for different groups? What rules shall we have for this group?

It is natural to want to feel accepted and liked. Feeling part of a group and being accepted and appreciated by a group gives us a sense of belonging and helps us to feel good about ourselves. But sometimes we can find ourselves behaving in ways that don't feel right just so we can be part of a group because we think it's 'cool' or it's exciting. There may be times when this is okay and also times when it's not okay, when trying to fit in leads to feeling awkward or unhappy. Then we have to be strong and make a different choice.

4. I like my hands because...

Wellbeing focus:

☑ Self-awareness   ☑ Self and others

Examples of personal skills learned or consolidated:

☑ Focusing attention   ☑ Observation

Examples of general/social learning:

☑ Development of body awareness and positive body image

☑ Developing self-respect and respect for others

☑ Appreciating diversity

This is also a useful activity to use early on in the life of a group, as it indicates to the children that we have a belief in their capabilities. The expansion activities emphasize the idea that children already have many different skills that could help them to understand and manage difficult feelings. This is then explored further in the next game, '5. Skill swap'. (See Chapter 5, 'Making Experience Count', in *Using Imagination, Mindful Play and Creative Thinking to Support Wellbeing and Resilience in Children* for more ideas about identifying and using current skills.)

How to play
Each child draws round his or her own hand. In each finger they write why they like their hands – for example, my hands are clever, creative, beautiful, strong, fast-moving. In the palm they write one thing that their hands enable them to do – play the keyboard, cut up food, stroke the cat.

Display the hand pictures for the children to guess the artist.

Adaptations

- Ask the children to 'introduce' their hands to the rest of the group and to say something about them.

- Younger children could cut out magazine pictures to show things they like to do with their hands.
- Make foot drawings and face drawings (a portrait frame and a magic mirror template are both available in Appendix C in *Using Imagination, Mindful Play and Creative Thinking to Support Wellbeing and Resilience in Children*). What do your feet help you to do? What does your face help you to do?

Talk about

What differences and similarities can you notice between the drawings? Have you ever really looked at your hands closely and noticed the patterns of lines, the skin colour, the way your fingers move? Do you mostly use your left hand or your right hand? Or do you use both? Do you mostly kick a ball with your right foot or your left foot, or both? Is this a difference or a skill?

EXPANSION ACTIVITY 4.1. SKILLS WHEEL

Ask the children to each think of something that they love to do and what skills they have that help them to love doing this. They then draw or write about these skills in their own skills wheel (see activity sheet 4.1).

This is a good activity to do in a group. By combining children's responses and writing them up on an extra large 'group wheel' you will be able to highlight a greater range of useful skills. You could also extend the metaphor by talking about how a steering wheel can help us to get where we are going. Perhaps several personal skills wheels working together (as on a bus) would be very helpful for a group project.

Talk about

How can these skills help us in other ways? (For example, a child might identify perseverance, ball control or speed as things that help them to enjoy a sport. These can then be 'mapped' on to other situations such as persevering with a difficult task, controlling a focus of attention and being able to control impulsive reactions to a difficult situation, as if having a speed control or a set of gears on a bike.)

Everyone has valuable skills and attributes. What skill or attribute are you most proud of? What is the difference between boasting and being proud about something? (Boasting and 'putting others down' can be how some children express anger when their own feelings of self-worth are low.)

Note: During all discussions it is helpful to use language that reflects the assumption that children are already doing something (however small) to help themselves to manage difficult emotions.

EXPANSION ACTIVITY 4.2. PRAISE

Complete activity sheet 4.2 together.
    This could also be used as an expansion activity for '12. If we were buildings'.

Talk about

What does it feel like to give and receive praise? How many different ways can we praise each other? What would you most like to be praised for? What do you think your mother/brother/best friend would most like to be praised for? Is there anything you don't like to be praised for?

5. Skill swap

Wellbeing focus:

☑ Self-awareness   ☑ Self and others

Examples of personal skills learned or consolidated:

☑ Negotiating   ☑ Sharing

☑ Cooperation   ☑ Making decisions

Examples of general/social learning:

☑ Awareness of different perspectives   ☑ Appreciation of personal and group skills

The adaptation for this game requires some preparation beforehand. There should be no element of win or lose in this game. The main emphasis is on how the players are able to negotiate and cooperate, how sets of skills are needed for different activities and how the same skills can be used in a variety of circumstances. Begin by talking about how this game is connected to '4. I like my hands because...' and 'Expansion activity 4.1. Skills wheel'.

How to play

The group is divided into two teams. Each team is given a large sheet of paper on which to make a collage or painting to represent a theme such as 'sport' or 'music'. Team A is given all the materials needed for the activity (coloured paper, paint, etc.) but no equipment. Team B is given all the equipment (paint brushes, scissors, glue, sticky tape, etc.) but no collage materials. The two teams need to negotiate with each other in order to make their collages.

Adaptation

- You will need to make a list of about 20 different skills such as observation, coordination, listening, memory, focusing attention and so on. This list is left on display for players to refer to throughout the game. Make a second copy on card that can be cut up into separate skills. Shuffle the cards and divide them equally between two teams of players. Each team needs skills for tasks that are very different to each other – for example, Team A has 'Playing football' and Team B has 'Walking a dog', or Team A has 'Organizing a group outing' and Team B has 'Cutting up vegetables'. The teams check through their cards and decide which skills they want to keep for their task. They then decide what they don't need. Now they take turns to negotiate a skill swap with the other team. The children work out the best way to do this, but if they are struggling, you could suggest examples such as 'We need listening skills. We can give you skills for research'. The other team then confer but might respond with 'No, we need listening skills because... [they need to give a valid reason], but we can give you observation skills'. Or 'Yes, you can have listening skills, but only if you give us memory strategies'. Each team has a maximum of five opportunities for swaps. You could also consider having some spare duplicate cards that teams could request after their five swaps.

Talk about

What happened during the trading? What worked? What didn't work? How might this game help players to manage difficult feelings? What skills are needed for negotiating and cooperating as a group? What do you think is one of your best skills?

Note: The most effective way of completing this task would be for both teams to cooperate with each other from the start. They could, for example, pool all their cards and then share them out appropriately. What would prevent this from happening? What would help this to happen?

6. Fruit salad

Wellbeing focus:

☑ Self-awareness ☑ Self and others

Examples of personal skills learned or consolidated:

☑ Focusing attention   ☑ Observation
☑ Listening   ☑ Taking turns
☑ Concentration   ☑ Categorizing
☑ Memory strategies

Examples of general/social learning:

☑ Developing self-respect and respect for others
☑ Appreciating diversity

☑ Understanding rules and how rules for games are made and can be changed

This is a well-known fast-paced game that can easily be adapted to suit different likes and dislikes. For this reason it can be played many times in different formats and is always a favourite among groups of active children. The expansion activity then invites children to experience the opposite of hectic activity by bringing them into a calm, focused space where they can explore different senses. The next game, '7. All birds fly', also promotes focusing skills and the ability to tolerate frustration.

How to play

Players sit in a circle with one person standing in the centre. Each person chooses the name of a different fruit. The person in the centre calls out two fruits. These two children swap places and the caller tries to sit in one of their seats before the other person gets there. If the caller says 'fruit salad' everyone swaps seats! The person left standing is the next caller.

Adaptations

- The children could swap chairs if they have something in common, such as cereal for breakfast this morning, brown eyes, etc. Everyone swaps when the caller says something that they know everyone has in common, such as 'Everyone who is wearing shoes (or doesn't have shoes on!)' or 'Everyone who is in Year 5'.

- Play the same game using car names for a motorway game or animal names for a zookeeper game – or anything else that comes in groups!
- For larger groups and a younger age range, have a limited number of items so that there is more than one child for each one (four apples, four bananas, etc.). This reduces the memory load, but it can get quite hectic with lots of children running across the circle at the same time, so take care!

Talk about

Do different children like different versions of the game? Why? Why can some games be frustrating for some players? What do all the games have in common? What are the rules for this game? Do all games have rules? Debate the pros and cons of competitive games and cooperative games.

What were you feeling/thinking when you were waiting to hear the person in the middle call out your chosen fruit?

EXPANSION ACTIVITY 6.1. FRUIT FOCUS

Have a small piece of fruit for each child. Instead of eating it quickly, ask the children to first spend time looking at the fruit and describing its colour, shape, texture and smell. Then invite them to take tiny bites and to hold the fruit in their mouth, really savouring the texture and taste. They do this silently so that all their concentration is on the sensation of eating. When they have finished, ask them to describe their experience of eating in such a focused way.

Try a different textured fruit. How are the sensations different? How are they the same?

Talk about

Did anything surprise you about this activity? How difficult or easy was it to only think about that particular piece of fruit? Did you have other thoughts while you were eating?

It is very normal to have other thoughts when you are putting your focus of attention onto one thing. You might be eating the fruit and noticing how it feels in your mouth and then suddenly you have a thought about what you will do after school, or you notice that the sun is shining outside, and you want to go and play. When that happens you can just notice it and then go back to focusing on eating the fruit. Your brain is very good at helping you to focus and re-focus. Practising this will help you to concentrate on bigger tasks too.

Learning to focus on an object or a sound or the sensation of your own breathing can be really helpful when you want to feel calm. Does anyone already have a way of calming their mind when they feel a bit wound up? There are lots of different ways to do this. Playing these games together in a group is helping you to try out different strategies. Is there anything that group members have shared today that you might try?

7. All birds fly

Wellbeing focus:

☑ Self-awareness ☑ Self and others

Examples of personal skills learned or consolidated:

☑ Focusing attention ☑ Self-control
☑ Listening ☑ Categorizing
☑ Concentration ☑ Tolerating frustration
☑ Observation

Example of general/social learning:

☑ Reducing impulsivity and
building persistence

This is a version of 'Simon says'. As with '6. Fruit salad', you could use this game to lead into a discussion about focusing attention and noticing, then diverting, your thoughts from unhelpful self-talk. The expansion activity offers an opportunity to discuss the links between focusing attention and concentrating for longer periods (see Chapter 7, 'Helping Children to Be Mindful', in *Using Imagination, Mindful Play and Creative Thinking to Support Wellbeing and Resilience in Children*).

How to play

The aim is for the caller to 'catch players off guard' by getting them to flap their arms at the wrong time. A chosen player starts the game by flapping their arms like a bird and saying 'all birds fly'. All other players in the group flap their arms in response. The caller then names a mixture of birds, animals and objects in random order, flapping their arms every time, for example 'eagles fly', 'sparrows fly', 'monkeys fly', 'chairs fly', 'crows fly'. The rest of the group should only flap their arms when a bird is called. If any player flaps when an animal or an object is called, they stand still for the next two calls. Each caller has three turns before handing over to another caller.

Adaptations

- The same game could be played as 'all fish swim'. The caller makes a 'swimming fish' gesture.
- The time for 'standing still' can be extended so that children experience waiting for longer periods.

Talk about

Was this easy or difficult? What helped you to control your responses? What were you feeling when you were waiting to join in again? What were you thinking? Did you notice if there was more than one person waiting at the same time? (If you didn't notice, that's okay.) What does that show us about this game? How can focusing games like this one help you to 'catch' unhelpful thoughts and let them go?

The most effective way to control the impulse to move is to only listen to the caller's words and not look at their actions or the actions of other children. Did anyone try to do this? How difficult or easy was this?

EXPANSION ACTIVITY 7.1. (UN-NAMED)

Players sit in a circle and someone is chosen to start off a mime sequence. They make a simple gesture such as clapping once, touching their ear or winking. The next player repeats this and adds a different gesture. This is a surprisingly difficult observation and sequencing game that can be made even more complex by having players keep their eyes closed until the person next to them taps them on the shoulder and shows them the sequence.

I have seen various names for this game, but here's an opportunity for children to invent their own title and also to see how many different versions they can think of. For example, add a vowel sound or add facial expressions. What would they call these versions?

8. Imagining

This activity gives children a basic introduction to using their imagination in a helpful way. This theme is expanded on throughout this book, and so the activity is not paired with any other specific game or activity.

Read 'Think of a chocolate cake' from activity sheet 8.1 slowly, with plenty of pauses for the children to really explore the images. Whenever possible, ask for verbal feedback while you are doing imagery exercises. For example, when you say 'What does it [the cake] look like?', the group can be asked to describe the sort of chocolate cake they are imagining. Repeat back what you have heard the child say or make some appropriate sound ('Mmmmmm!'). The interaction might go something like:

'You see the cake on a big plate… Would anyone like to say what their chocolate cake looks like?'

'It's got chocolate sprinkles on.'

'Simon's cake has chocolate sprinkles.'

'Squidgy.'

'Mmmm – a squidgy cake for Craig.'

When you have finished, discuss the similarities and differences in the responses. Reassure the children that there are no right or wrong answers. If anyone seems unable to 'see' images, that's okay. In my experience, however, children are usually very quick to produce visual images.

Adaptations

- Older children might enjoy imagining themselves achieving in sport or eating their favourite meal.
- One image that works well in engendering a physical response is to imagine eating a slice of lemon. If you encourage children to see, smell and feel a lemon in their imagination, and then to imagine chewing a slice of it,

you will probably find that any child who has previously tasted one has an almost instant rush of saliva!

Talk about

Sometimes we can experience a feeling just by imagining something. Have you ever felt cross about something that hasn't happened yet or something that happened a long time ago, but you keep imagining it over again? What about happy feelings? Have you ever felt happy when you are thinking about something that *might* happen or when you think about being in a favourite place? We can use our imagination to help us to do all sorts of things like solve problems, set goals, relax, re-energize, build skills, make important changes, cope with difficulties. We can also use our imagination to change the way that our body feels when we are tired or cross or fed up.

Sometimes just thinking about a person or an object or a calm place can help us to feel calm and more in control of our feelings.

Working Together

By doing the activities in this section you will be helping children to:

- continue to build or consolidate self-respect and respect for others
- build or consolidate skills of cooperation, building trust and understanding empathy
- build or consolidate their ability to share responsibility for group effectiveness and problem-solving.

9. Big group yell

Wellbeing focus:

☑ Self-awareness   ☑ Self and others

Examples of personal skills learned or consolidated:

☑ Listening   ☑ Taking turns
☑ Self-calming   ☑ Cooperation
☑ Self-control

Examples of general/social learning:

☑ Awareness of others   ☑ Group cohesion

This is often suggested as a celebratory activity at the end of a course. I like to use the basic activity and the adapted versions as ways of releasing energy as well, to show in a very quick and easy way how a group of individuals can come together in a shared activity that is fun and safe. The following activity, '10. Big ball parachute game', and its expansion activity provide an opportunity to further explore the concept of group cohesion.

How to play
Players crouch down together in a close group. The game coordinator starts off a low humming sound and the others join in. As the whole group gradually stands up, the noise level gets louder and louder until everyone jumps into the air and yells as loudly as they can.

Adaptations

- Players crouch down in a circle facing inwards. Everyone hums quietly and then gradually gets louder as they all stand up together and raise their arms above their heads. Then everyone does the reverse – starting with a loud hum and getting quieter and quieter as they sink down to the ground. Then they lie down with their feet towards the centre of the circle in complete silence.

- Half fill a variety of recycled plastic pots or small cardboard containers with beads, buttons or play sand and seal them tightly to make shakers. Use these shakers to make a crescendo of noise by adding on one person at a time, and then stop one person at a time until there is silence.

Talk about

Introduce or expand on the concept of a group having a beginning and an end point. Encourage the children to think about what it is like to share experiences in groups and how group games can help us to feel energized and full of confidence. Think about building energy for action and the usefulness of 'winding down' or chilling.

Notice and appreciate the way in which members of a group can all cooperate to change the intensity of a sound at the same time.

What motivates you? Can you think of five 'free' motivators (no money involved!)? Possible ideas might be praise, extra time for play, feeling good about achieving something, someone important noticing that you're trying to stay calm, enjoying friendships more and so on.

Note: Children are much more likely to be motivated to make changes if they can see the personal relevance of doing so (see the accompanying eBook Using Imagination, Mindful Play and Creative Thinking to Support Wellbeing and Resilience in Children*).*

EXPANSION ACTIVITY 9.1. IMAGINE

Imagine that it is the end of the day/week/term and you are feeling really good about everything that you have achieved. What did you do to help you to feel this way? What skills and qualities did you use? Imagine that your friends are congratulating you. What are they saying? How do you feel now?

Imagining something as if it has already happened helps your mind to make a 'memory'. This can sometimes be more powerful than making a plan. Does anyone know how this type of imagining is used in sports? (See the accompanying eBook *Using Imagination, Mindful Play and Creative Thinking to Support Wellbeing and Resilience in Children*.)

10. Big ball parachute game

Wellbeing focus:

☑ Self-awareness ☑ Self and others

Examples of personal skills learned or consolidated:

☑ Cooperation ☑ Taking turns
☑ Observation

Example of general/social learning:

☑ Understanding different
perspectives

(See also '9. Big group yell'.)

How to play

Players stand in a circle and hold the parachute at waist level and send a very large ball around the circle. One half of the players aim to try and keep the ball in the circle while the other half try and send it out.

Adaptation

- Players send several different-sized balls around the circle, either with everyone cooperating to try to keep the balls going in the same direction, or with half the group trying to send the balls out of the circle.

Talk about

How easy or difficult is it to cooperate in a large group? What about in a small group of just three or four people? What are some of the real-life situations where groups of children might need to cooperate? What happens when some members of the group find it difficult to cooperate? What skills are needed for maintaining cooperation? Is it helpful or not helpful for group members to each take on different tasks? Is it helpful or not helpful to have a leader? Why do you think this?

EXPANSION ACTIVITY 10.1. GROUP DRAWING

Set out large sheets of paper on tables so that groups of children can move around their table easily. Each group draws a collaborative picture or just makes 'marks' on the paper, using a variety of pencils, pastels and pens. The group coordinator can provide a theme or leave the children to draw whatever they like.

Adaptation

- Draw pictures in pairs. Divide a piece of paper in two so that pairs can draw at the same time or take turns.

Talk about

What does it feel like to draw a joint picture? How did you feel when someone drew their image very close to yours or changed your image in some way? What are some of the differences between all drawing different things on the same piece of paper and all drawing a truly collaborative picture?

11. Walk this way

Wellbeing focus:

☑ Self-awareness ☑ Self and others

Examples of personal skills learned or consolidated:

☑ Focusing attention ☑ Taking turns
☑ Concentration ☑ Understanding same/different
☑ Observation

Examples of general/social learning:

☑ Developing self-respect and respect for others ☑ Dramatic awareness
☑ Development of body awareness and positive body image
☑ Appreciating diversity
☑ Understanding empathy

The ability to imagine is an important aspect of empathy. This introduces the idea of 'walking in someone else's shoes', and the next activity, '12. If we were buildings', focuses on awareness of how we might perceive others and how others might perceive us. Exploring concepts of empathy and respect will ease the process of talking about different emotions and personal experiences in the group.

How to play

The game coordinator asks a 'leader' to walk around the room in a chosen way, for example like a giant like the world's strongest person or like an older person who has stiff joints. Everyone watches closely and then tries to walk in exactly the same way. When the game coordinator rings a bell or bangs a drum, everyone 'freezes' in one position. They hold this position for the count of five. Then someone else leads the group in a different type of walk until the game coordinator rings the bell again. Continue for at least five different walks.

Adaptations

- Walk in different ways to reflect different emotions.
- In pairs, try and exactly mirror how your partner walks across the room.

Talk about

Think about similarities and differences in the ways that people walk. What about the other children in your group/class? How are you all different from each other? Are there any ways in which you are all the same? (Think about such things as looks, actions, likes and dislikes.) What would the world be like if we all talked and moved in exactly the same way? What would it be like if we all hated/loved the same food? Why would that be difficult? And *then* what would happen? See 'Talk about' suggestions for '3. Sort us out'.

How does it feel to 'walk in someone else's shoes'? How does it feel when someone else really tries to feel what it is like to be you?

In this game players imagined what it would be like to be someone else. Do you think the ability to imagine is useful? Why do you think that? How has it helped you so far?

12. If we were buildings

Wellbeing focus:

☑ Self-awareness   ☑ Self and others

Examples of personal skills learned or consolidated:

☑ Memory strategies   ☑ Observation
☑ Listening   ☑ Understanding metaphors

Examples of general/social learning:

☑ Building trust   ☑ Understanding empathy
☑ Developing sensitivity to   ☑ Developing self-respect and
  other people's strengths and   respect for others
  differences

(See also '11. Walk this way'.)

This game will highlight how well the group now know each other. It is helpful if the group talks about positive perceptions before the first player leaves the room. Encourage the children to recognize and praise listening and observation skills, and respect and empathy shown by each other. The importance of genuine praise is explored in 'Expansion activity 4.2. Praise'. If you have not already done this activity you could use it here or perhaps revisit it.

How to play
Players sit in a circle. Player One leaves the room and the others choose someone in the group who will be described. Player One returns to the room and is allowed to ask ten questions in order to find out who the group have chosen. Each question must take the form of 'If this person were a _____ [building, house, car, bird, etc.] what kind of _____ [building, house, car, bird, etc.] would they be?' When Player One guesses correctly, another person leaves the room and the process is repeated.

Adaptations

- Instead of leaving the room, Player One is blindfolded. The game coordinator silently chooses who will be the first person to be guessed. Player One then removes their blindfold.
- Instead of choosing a person, the group chooses an emotion for Player One to guess.

Talk about

We all have many different aspects to our personality. Sometimes the way that other people see us is different to how we see ourselves. Why do you think this might happen? In what ways does this affect how you feel about yourself or about other people? Why do you think this? What would be helpful in this situation (when you feel that someone has misunderstood something about you)?

Anger is only one of many emotions that we are capable of experiencing. Feeling angry about specific things is not the same as being an 'angry person'. What are some of the other emotions that you feel every day?

13. Green space group tag

Wellbeing focus:

☑ Self-awareness   ☑ Self and others

Examples of personal skills learned or consolidated:

☑ Observation   ☑ Self-control
☑ Cooperation   ☑ Giving instructions
☑ Physical coordination

Examples of general/social learning:

☑ Developing sensitivity to   ☑ Building trust
other people's strengths and   ☑ Understanding different
differences   perspectives

The unadapted game requires plenty of space and a high level of cooperation. The ideal location would be outside in a flat field, where there are no trip hazards, but small groups could play this indoors in a sports hall, for example. The adapted version can be played in a smaller space. The next activity, '14. Blind walk', is similar to the adapted version of this tag game, but requires players to take greater shared responsibility.

How to play

The game starts in the same way as a normal tag game. The first player to be the 'tagger' runs after the rest of the group. When they manage to tag another player they join hands. These two players then try to tag a third and then a fourth player who also join up with them. As soon as there is a group of four players together, they split into two sets and each set goes off to tag two more players until there is only one person left who has not yet been tagged. If the game is to continue, this player starts off as the new tagger.

Adaptation

• The group find their own space in a large room and stand very still until they are tagged. One player is blindfolded and is the first tagger. This player is helped by the game coordinator who can give directions such as 'two steps to your left, go straight' and so on. When the tagger finds someone (Player Two), they hold hands and continue to walk around the room looking for a third player to tag. This time Player Two gives directions to Player One. When a third player is tagged, the task becomes more difficult. Player Three now holds hands with Players One and Two to form a line or a circle (depending on the players' abilities). Player Three gives instructions to Player One. Player Two might find themselves moving backwards and so must keep a careful watch. Once again, when four players meet, they split into two groups and one player from each of these groups is given a blindfold. Now the instructors have to take note of other groups as well, so that no one bumps into anyone else. Play can continue until everyone is part of a group.

Talk about

This game only works well if players cooperate fully with each other and are careful with how they move.

In the *unadapted version*, was it difficult or easy for small groups to cooperate? How did you decide in which direction to run? Were you all trying to run at the same pace? What were the small groups trying to do? Was it important to stay together or to catch someone else? Did any leaders emerge? If so, how did they lead? How did other group members respond?

In the *adapted version*, what did it feel like to have responsibility for giving directions? What did it feel like to be led by someone else? What were you feeling and thinking while you were waiting to be tagged?

14. Blind walk

Wellbeing focus:

☑ Self-awareness   ☑ Self and others

Examples of personal skills learned or consolidated:

☑ Giving instructions   ☑ Self-control
☑ Observation   ☑ Leadership
☑ Physical coordination

Examples of general/social learning:

☑ Understanding responsibility for   ☑ Building trust
  others   ☑ Understanding empathy

(See also '13. Green space group tag'.)

This game also requires plenty of space for players to move around in. A few large obstacles can be used for players to negotiate.

How to play

Divide the group into two. One half of the group will act as silent 'protectors', while the other half of the group, the 'explorers', is led on a blind walk. The protectors will gently prevent the explorers from walking into obstacles or each other (by touching them on the arm if they get too close, for example). The explorers choose one leader whom they trust to lead them around the room in a snake formation (with the leader as the head of the snake). Each explorer puts one hand on the shoulder of the person in front of them. The game coordinator, the protectors and the line leader all keep their eyes open. The leader can give verbal instructions. Everyone else in the snake has their eyes shut.

Adaptations

- Mark out three sides of a large enclosure on the floor. A 'shepherd' tries to round up a group of blindfolded children ('sheep') and move them into the pen one at a time using only four words – forwards, backwards, left, right – and a whistle to indicate the number of steps to take.

- Players work in pairs and help their partner to 'explore' their surroundings through touch. They can progress from holding their partner's arm, to touching an elbow, to just touching fingertips.

Talk about

What did you discover? What helped you to feel safe? Was it the reassurance of the leader? Precise directions? Tone of voice? Did you feel able to ask the leader to slow down if needed? What did it feel like to be the leader? Were you aware of how the rest of the snake was coping with the blind walk? Do you think you gave clear instructions?

In what way is your imagination useful in this game? How might this game help you to understand another person's point of view?

15. Talking heads

Wellbeing focus:

☑ Self-awareness ☑ Self and others

Examples of personal skills learned or consolidated:

☑ Cooperation   ☑ Sequencing
☑ Taking turns   ☑ Asking and answering questions
☑ Concentration

Examples of general/social learning:

☑ Reducing impulsivity   ☑ Understanding different perspectives

This links with '16. Story-telling'. Both activities explore the ability to understand different perspectives.

How to play

In pairs, children put one arm round each other and act as if they were one person. They talk about a given subject, with each person saying one word at a time to make sentences. This means that they have to guess what the other person is aiming to say and it can get quite frustrating and difficult! Topics could include 'Why I like chocolate', 'What I did yesterday', 'My favourite holiday' and 'What I learned at school this morning'.

Adaptation

- The audience asks questions and the pair has to answer one word at a time.

Talk about

Was this easy or difficult? Did the pairs manage to cooperate to make sense, even if they couldn't guess what their partner was going to say? Sometimes we think we know what other people are thinking. Sometimes we expect others to know what *we* are thinking! How can we help others to understand our perspectives? What can we do to help us to understand someone else's viewpoint?

16. Story-telling

Wellbeing focus:

☑ Self-awareness   ☑ Self and others

Examples of personal skills learned or consolidated:

☑ Sequencing/story-telling   ☑ Problem-solving

Examples of general/social learning:

☑ Reducing impulsivity   ☑ Understanding different perspectives

(See also '15. Talking heads'.)

I suggest that at least for the first round the players choose the 'problem'. The next round could then be directly related to a situation involving a potentially angry exchange that is successfully averted.

How to play

In a circle, the first player starts off a story by stating a 'problem' that needs to be solved. The next player continues the story by saying one or two sentences. The third player adds one or two more sentences and so on, around the circle. The aim is for the last person in the circle to bring the story to a satisfactory conclusion while still only using two sentences at the most.

A new problem is then introduced. The game continues for as long as all players remain engaged.

Adaptation

- The group is given a selection of catchphrases or objects that must be incorporated into the story in a cohesive way. Players may choose these at random or they have to follow a pattern, such as 'every third person in the circle picks an object to include in their part of the story'. The game coordinator can challenge unconvincing connections.

Talk about

Was this easy or difficult? Were players helping each other out? If so, how did they do that?

Were there creative solutions to problems?

Does it help to have more than one person solving a problem? Did other players have different solutions that they didn't have the chance to share?

How can your imagination help you to be creative? Do you think that inventors are good at imagining? Why do you think this?

IV

Exploring Emotions and Degrees of Emotion

By doing the activities in this section you will be helping children to:

- identify different emotions and explore the ways in which we express these
- identify different degrees of emotion
- explore the idea that feelings can change and that they can have some control over them
- understand that what they think affects how they feel and what they do
- understand what happens to them physically when they have a strong emotion such as anger
- explore strategies for relieving uncomfortable feelings associated with anger.

17. Ladder of feelings

Wellbeing focus:

☑ Self-awareness   ☑ Self and others

Examples of personal skills learned or consolidated:

☑ Understanding emotions   ☑ Focusing attention
☑ Cooperation   ☑ Concentration
☑ Negotiating   ☑ Categorizing

Examples of general/social learning:

☑ Developing self-respect and respect for others   ☑ Building trust

This is a well-known activity about recognizing other people's emotions and noting similarities and differences in degrees of emotion. You will need to make enough large wall charts for the number of groups playing plus one extra. Each chart should have four giant ladders drawn on it – one for each emotional theme. The next activity, '18. Hands up!', continues this theme.

How to play

Groups are given a time limit in which to think of as many feeling words as possible within the four themes of 'anger', 'fear', 'sadness' and 'joy'. Each word is written on separate cards. Players in each group then decide between themselves where each feeling word should be placed on the ladders. For example 'furious' and 'annoyed' would be placed on the 'anger' ladder, but 'annoyed' would be near the bottom of the ladder and 'furious' would be higher up. Groups then combine to negotiate making a final wall chart to show all the feelings in an agreed order.

Adaptations

- Mark out a long line on the floor to indicate a scale of 1 to 10. Groups of children choose a category and then each child picks one of the words from that category. They then arrange themselves in order of intensity along the line.

- Once the cards have been arranged in order of intensity, place them on the floor and ask the children to line up behind the level of emotion that they feel most confident about coping with. For example: 'If this was a level 5 confidence, where would you put yourself for a level 4?' Confidence level 5 might be coping with mild frustration and 4 might be coping with feeling annoyed.

- If you have a big space for games, make this into an active game by designating each of the four sides of a room or playground as a different emotion. Put cards numbered 1 to 5 along each of the four sides (these represent the intensity of the emotion – for example, 1 might be 'slightly' happy/sad/angry/afraid and 5 might be 'very' happy/sad/angry/afraid). Call out different scenarios, such as 'You drop your lunch', 'You win a trophy', 'You see your best friend being bullied' and so on. Children run to the different sides and different numbers. Again, reassure them that there is no right or wrong response for this particular game; it is about identifying emotions and looking for similarities and differences. However, if any children want to change their mind about where they place themselves, they can be given the opportunity to do so.

Talk about

Were there any disagreements about levels of emotions? Do some children experience emotions near the top of the ladders a lot of the time? How can we recognize different levels of similar emotions in ourselves and in others?

Imagine if each degree of emotion was represented by a colour, what colour would 'furious' be? What colour would 'cross' be? What about 'excited'? 'Happy'? 'Overjoyed'? 'Sad'?

18. Hands up!

Wellbeing focus:

☑ Self-awareness   ☑ Self and others

Examples of personal skills learned or consolidated:

☑ Focusing attention   ☑ Listening

Examples of general/social learning:

☑ Developing self-respect and   ☑ Dramatic awareness
respect for others   ☑ Flexibility of thought

(See also '17. Ladder of feelings'.)

This game can be based on any emotion, for example degrees of happiness or anxiety. Players need to stand in a large enough space so that they have room to move their arms and hands without touching anyone else.

How to play

Demonstrate how we can move our arms freely in the air and at the same time shake our hands loosely. When all players are moving freely, the game coordinator calls out a word that reflects a degree of anger (for example, 'annoyed', 'frustrated', 'furious', 'cross'). Players begin an angry conversation between their two hands. After 30 seconds the coordinator calls 'hands up'. Players raise their hands above their heads and stretch as high as they can go. The coordinator then calls another anger word and players drop their arms down and act out another conversation between their hands until the coordinator calls 'hands up' again. Continue for at least four levels of anger, and then finish with a calm conversation. Instead of 'hands up' at the end, the coordinator calls 'handshake'. Players shake hands with themselves!

Adaptation

- Invent a 'hand dance' changing from calm to angry and back again. In small groups players can take turns to demonstrate their hand dance or to teach it to the rest of the group.

Talk about

Did you feel any tightness or tension in your body during this game? Are there times when our hands show how we are feeling? If our hands are tense, does anything happen to the rest of our body?

Even small changes in body tension and posture (for example, unclenching your jaw or relaxing your hands) can make a big difference to how we feel and to how other people *think* we feel. Can you think of postures that look nearly the same but mean something very different?

How do you stand or sit when you are feeling angry? How do other people know when you are feeling angry? What is the smallest thing that you need to do or to say for other people to know how you are feeling?

When you are not feeling angry, what *are* you feeling? How do other people know that you are feeling this way?

19. Emotion masks

Wellbeing focus:

☑ Self-awareness   ☑ Self and others

Examples of personal skills learned or consolidated:

☑ Focusing attention   ☑ Taking turns
☑ Concentration   ☑ Understanding and using non-
☑ Observation   verbal communication

Examples of general/social learning:

☑ Developing self-respect and   ☑ Building trust
   respect for others   ☑ Dramatic awareness
☑ Understanding empathy

In this game players begin to think about indicators of emotions in more detail. In the expansion activity, they are invited to think about their own indicators of emotions and some of the aspects of emotions that others may be unaware of. This also links with '20. Creative emotions'.

How to play
Players sit in a circle. The first player 'pulls a face' to show a strong emotion, then 'removes' the face with their hands as if it were a mask and passes it to the player on their left. This player 'puts on' the mask, copying the expression as accurately as possible. The second player then changes the expression and passes it on to the next person and so on, around the circle.

Adaptations

- Introduce a limited number of options to pass around the circle, for example happy, sad, angry. All the children practise these first.
- Limit the part of the mask that can be altered, for example only the eyes and eyebrows, or just the mouth.

Talk about

Which masks did players think they were putting on? What emotions did players pass to others? Did these match up? If not, why do you think that happened? Is it possible to show an emotion with just one part of the face? Were there different degrees of any similar emotions passed around (for example, happy/ excited)? How do we show different degrees of emotion (for example, by facial expression, posture, actions)?

EXPANSION ACTIVITY 19.1. LOOK OUT FOR ICEBERGS

Facilitate a group discussion about how little or how much we reveal our emotions and thoughts. This can be likened to an iceberg. For example, some 'under the surface' aspects of a difficulty may be displayed overtly although not necessarily in a way that might be expected. Embarrassment may 'appear' in the form of verbal aggression, or anger might appear above the surface as being tearful or looking flushed. Think about this as a whole group. Explore a range of feelings such as excitement, embarrassment, sadness and feeling scared. How many different emotions can the group think of that might 'look' like anger or frustration? How many different signs of genuine anger might be displayed above the surface?

Each child can then select the relevant elements to write or draw on their own iceberg (activity sheet 19.1). This can be used as a self-help tool at a later date. For example, as some elements are reduced or eliminated, there will be a natural effect on others, so the iceberg can be redrawn. The children can then compare the different versions of their own icebergs at different stages. One of the major bonuses of group work for children is the opportunity it provides for sharing feelings and insights. Realizing that other children think or feel the same way about a similar challenge can be very affirming. I have found that the iceberg activity can be particularly useful in this respect.

Talk about

What happens when we forget that there are large parts of an iceberg under the surface of the water? It is not helpful to ignore an iceberg. It *is* helpful to know more about it. This also links with '20. Creative emotions'.

20. Creative emotions

Wellbeing focus:

☑ Self-awareness   ☑ Self and others

Examples of personal skills learned or consolidated:

☑ Focusing attention   ☑ Understanding and using non-verbal communication
☑ Observation
☑ Taking turns

Examples of general/social learning:

☑ Developing self-respect and respect for others   ☑ Building trust
☑ Dramatic awareness
☑ Understanding empathy

(See also '19. Emotion masks'.)

This game can be played to help children to make links between feelings, thoughts and actions.

How to play

The game coordinator suggests different emotions and all the children try to show these emotions in any non-verbal way they can think of, for example as an animal, as a movement, by facial expression or the way they walk. The coordinator shouts 'freeze' and everyone 'holds' the pose and feels what it's like for a few seconds.

The children shake that feeling out of their body (shaking their arms, hands and legs), and then try a different emotion. They should finish with at least two positive emotions.

Adaptation

- The children act out actions and feelings together randomly such as doing the ironing sadly, eating a sandwich happily.

Talk about

Sometimes we can be saying one thing and feeling something completely different. Does our body language sometimes 'give the game away'? If someone tells you they are angry but they are smiling, would you believe their words or their facial expression? When you 'freeze' your body during different emotions, what do you notice?

How do you usually show that you are angry? How do you usually show that you are happy or sad? How do you show that you are excited?

We can have different levels of the same feeling in different situations – like having a volume control or an intensity control – for example, we could be slightly frustrated when we make a mistake, and furious when someone accuses us of something that we didn't do (see '17. Ladder of feelings').

21. Waves on the sea parachute game

Wellbeing focus:

☑ Self-awareness ☑ Self and others

Examples of personal skills learned or consolidated:

☑ Focusing attention ☑ Physical coordination
☑ Concentration ☑ Cooperation
☑ Observation ☑ Listening
☑ Taking turns ☑ Self-control

Examples of general/social learning:

☑ Dramatic awareness ☑ Understanding why some rules are needed for safety

As with all games involving the use of equipment, parachute games need to be supervised by an adult at all times. Make it clear that parachutes must not be used to carry or bounce each other. This 'rule' can be a useful prompt for a discussion about why some rules are needed for safety reasons (see below).

Although parachute games are usually played in larger groups, they can often be adapted for two to three people to play by using any large piece of material, such as a round tablecloth.

How to play

Players stand in a circle, holding the parachute with both hands at waist level. A large soft ball is placed in the middle. The game coordinator gives instructions for how calm or stormy the waves on the 'sea' (the parachute) should be and players move the parachute accordingly while trying to stop the soft ball from falling off.

The game finishes with a calm rippling of the parachute, which is then gently laid on the ground. The children sit quietly on the edge of the 'sea'. This would be a good time to tell a story that has an anger theme. For example, tiger cubs coping with sibling rivalry, a wolf who bullies another member of the pack, a beaver who is so angry it breaks something important (perhaps a beaver dam)

and has to fix it. What strategies can the 'helper' in the story suggest? How is the situation resolved? (See the accompanying eBook *Using Imagination, Mindful Play and Creative Thinking to Support Wellbeing and Resilience in Children* for ideas about structuring wellbeing stories.)

Adaptations

- Use several smaller soft balls on the parachute.
- Tell the story of a storm building up on land from gentle rain to a tornado and then subsiding. Players move the parachute according to the strength of the wind.
- Players take turns to give instructions for moving the parachute at ground level (like rippling water, big waves, water flowing over rocks). Two or more players walk across the surface of the parachute in ways that match the movement.

Talk about

How easy or difficult was it to cooperate to keep the soft ball on the parachute? What happened to the soft balls when the sea was raging or the storm was strong?

Feelings can be like a stormy sea or a quiet sea. Difficult feelings can build and subside or can come on very suddenly and perhaps unexpectedly. Pleasant feelings come and go as well. This is normal.

What happens if our feelings get out of control? How might this affect us? How might it affect other people around us? What happens if one or two people in a group are 'making waves' when everyone else is being calm? Can you think of times when feeling angry is a useful emotion? What is the difference between feeling angry and acting in an angry way?

What is the difference between a rule, a law and a guideline? What 'rules' do we have in this group about preferred behaviour and unwanted behaviour? How might safety rules apply to managing angry feelings? For example, when we are angry, we don't hit others, we don't throw or break things, we don't hurt ourselves... Are you able to think of the positive alternatives for these three rules? For example, what would be a useful picture to have in your mind to replace 'don't hit others'?

Exploring Strategies for Emotion Regulation

By doing the activities in this section you will be helping children to:

- understand how they can develop control over the ways in which they manage strong emotions
- try out a variety of different self-calming strategies.

22. Sleeping giants

Wellbeing focus:

☑ Self-awareness   ☑ Self and others

Examples of personal skills learned or consolidated:

☑ Listening   ☑ Monitoring physical sensations
☑ Observation   ☑ Self-control
☑ Self-calming

Examples of general/social learning:

☑ Awareness of others   ☑ Reducing impulsivity

This game provides children with an opportunity to focus on and monitor physical sensations and is an introduction to '23. Shaping up!' and '24. In the hot seat'. The expansion activities offer two different ways of thinking about current skills and strategies for self-calming.

How to play

Players pretend to be giants. They stamp loudly around the room until the game coordinator gives a signal, such as ringing a small bell or raising one hand in the air. Then the giants lie down on the ground and close their eyes. The game coordinator walks quietly around the room to see if they are all 'asleep'. The coordinator can talk but must not touch the giants. If any giants are seen to move then they sit up and help to look for any others who are moving.

Adaptation

- Use two different types of music – one very loud with a heavy beat and one quiet and gentle. The giants move to the sound of the first and lie down when they hear the second; or they move more slowly to the gentle music and lie down when the music stops. Finish the game with a calm period when everyone is lying down or sitting quietly, listening to calm music or listening to a short story.

Talk about

How easy or difficult is it for you to stay still and calm?

How easy or difficult is it for you to be active and to listen or watch for a signal from someone else?

When the giants were stamping around, did anyone bump into another giant? Why do you think this happened?

Does your breathing change when you are being calm? How does it change? When might it be useful to make your breathing calm on purpose?

What did you discover that could help you when you are starting to feel angry?

EXPANSION ACTIVITY 22.1. I CAN CHANGE THE WAY I FEEL

Children can find it very hard to cope if their feelings change too frequently or too quickly. Take turns to think of ideas for what can be done to keep feelings balanced. This could be done now – to highlight any current skills and strategies – and again later, once children have learned or consolidated a range of different strategies. For example, if I keep getting cross/fed up/ irritated/furious (be specific), I can:

- tell someone what I'm feeling
- sit and do a quiet activity until I feel more calm
- go and scribble in a book kept just for this
- write down all the things that I'm angry about
- think about what I'm going to do later that I'm looking forward to
- daydream about what I'd like to happen: 'Wouldn't it be great if I could have that new game/stay up late/go to the park? If I was invisible/a giant/an adult, I would...'

The children make their own personal lists by using activity sheet 22.1 and tick them off when they've tried each strategy. What strategies have they already tried? What nearly happened? What happened instead?

EXPANSION ACTIVITY 22.2. TROUBLESOME TIGERS

Complete activity sheet 22.2 together.

Invite the children to contribute ideas. Think about strategies that they have tried and found to be helpful and those that they perhaps know about but have not tried or thought were unhelpful.

At the end of the discussion the children may want to add some more ideas to their activity sheet. Revisit these at a later point and see if anyone can report a success in following through with one of their ideas.

For example, younger children often benefit from help in directing their attention towards a pleasurable activity to soothe their anger. Older children may need the time to engage in an activity that they know will help them to 'cool off', such as going for a walk, reading quietly or listening to music. In a classroom situation a child's energy can be directed into doing something constructive or practical.

23. Shaping up!

Wellbeing focus:

☑ Self-awareness   ☑ Self and others

Examples of personal skills learned or consolidated:

☑ Focusing attention   ☑ Listening

☑ Concentration   ☑ Understanding opposites

Examples of general/social learning:

☑ Dramatic awareness   ☑ Extending awareness

This activity and the expansion activities extend the use of imagery by inviting children to allow their own images to 'emerge' from their imagination. It works best if children have already done '8. Imagining'. Remind the children that it is important to accept everyone's images in a respectful way. (See Chapter 9, 'Image-Making', in *Using Imagination, Mindful Play and Creative Thinking to Support Wellbeing and Resilience in Children* for further guidelines for using imagery, including an example of encouraging feedback in this activity.) Since anger itself is not always an unwanted emotion, a child's opposite might just be 'less angry' or 'controlled anger'. The next activity, '24. In the hot seat', takes this one step further in understanding the 'character' of anger and its opposite.

How to play

Invite the children to settle themselves into a comfortable position in their chairs or sitting on the floor. Read the following activity slowly, with plenty of pauses, to give them time to explore their images. Ask for feedback as appropriate – 'Would anyone like to tell us their image for anger?'

> Close your eyes and take three full breaths, letting the air out slowly as you breathe out...
>
> Allow your imagination to come up with an image for 'anger'...it might be a shape, an animal, a plant or an object...anything at all...just allow it to appear in your imagination... Now imagine that you could make this image out of modelling

clay... [Encourage the children to move their hands as if they were physically moulding the image into something that they could hold in one hand.] Which hand is it in? What does it look like?... Is it light or heavy?... What colour is it?... Does it make a sound? If so, what sound does it make? If this anger image had a name, what name would it have? Quick! Before it sets into that shape – mould it into the opposite of [name of the angry image]. Which hand is this new image in? What does it look like?... What does it feel like?... Does it make a sound? If so, what sound does it make? What name will you give this image? What would you like to do with [the image] now? When you are ready, open your eyes and give your arms and hands a shake. Now we're ready to create that!

EXPANSION ACTIVITY 23.1. CREATE THAT!

Maybe the children can really sculpt their own images or draw or paint them or make up a poem about them – invite them to be as creative as they like in how they record their images of anger and its opposite.

EXPANSION ACTIVITY 23.2. WHAT DOES ANGER FEEL LIKE?

Complete activity sheet 23.2 together. Talk about physical signs of rising anger (the body's fight or flight response). Note how it is possible to recognize these signs before they become too intense. Invite the children to draw a body outline and mark any areas of tension noted by them when they are angry. What have they noticed in other people?

Refer back to '23. Shaping up!' Talk about how we can be imagining an event so clearly that our body reacts as though that event was actually happening. We just think about a situation that made us feel angry or *might* make us feel angry and our body could start to tense up, ready for a fight.

A body focus exercise could be helpful here (see Appendix A in the accompanying eBook *Using Imagination, Mindful Play and Creative Thinking to Support Wellbeing and Resilience in Children*).

24. In the hot seat

Wellbeing focus:

☑ Self-awareness ☑ Self and others

Examples of personal skills learned or consolidated:

☑ Sharing information ☑ Understanding opposites
☑ Listening ☑ Answering questions

Examples of general/social learning:

☑ Dramatic awareness ☑ Exploring self-concept and
☑ Extending awareness   self-efficacy

Although hot-seating generally involves other children in the audience asking their own questions, this exercise is best facilitated by an adult. Alternatively, the audience could be given the questions and choose which one they will each ask.

How to play

The children are invited to 'hot-seat' their image of anger and then their image of the 'opposite of anger' (see '23. Shaping up!'), as if they were characters in a story. Volunteers sit in a pre-designated chair. It is a good idea to make this a chair that is not generally used by the children. They then answer questions from the facilitator as if they were their image. So, for example, they might introduce themselves as 'I am a mountain and I am called angry'. The facilitator then asks the following questions:

What size of mountain are you?

Were you always a mountain, or has there been a time when things were different?

What do you most like about being a mountain? Is there anything that you don't like about being a mountain?

What do you most wish for?

What are you really good at doing?

What advice or suggestions do you have for your audience?

The child, having answered as many of these questions as they feel happy to, then stands up, moves away from the chair, and steps out of the image by shaking their arms and legs, hands and feet and saying their own name and one thing they like to eat or what they are going to do later in the day.

They then move to another chair (again, one that is not generally used by children). They introduce themselves as their second image. Questions to this new 'image' are the same as before. Once again, when the child has answered as many questions as they feel happy to, they step out of this image, shake their body all over and say something that indicates they are back to being a child again.

The children can be encouraged to elaborate on their second image as much as possible so that they have a strong sense of what they are aiming for. If you do not have time for all the children to hot-seat their images, they might do this by writing a 'character sketch' for their image as if it was going to be in an animated cartoon, or apply the characteristics to a fictitious person and write a CV outlining their suitability for a job in an ice cream factory.

Talk about

Was this activity easy or difficult? Why was that? What suggestions did players make that might be helpful for others to try?

You have heard a lot of different ideas about anger. How might these ideas be helpful to you in the future?

Could this activity be useful for exploring any other emotions?

EXPANSION ACTIVITY 24.1. THE STORIES WE TELL (1)

If you have not already done so, this would be an ideal time to introduce children to wellbeing stories (see the accompanying eBook *Using Imagination, Mindful Play and Creative Thinking to Support Wellbeing and Resilience in Children*).

Each child writes or tells a story based on their image characters. They can ask to 'borrow' characters from other children, or three children could collaborate to make up a story. Remind the children that their story should involve a helper, a task to complete or a problem to solve and one or more obstacles to overcome. The story should end with a positive resolution.

VI

Causes and Consequences

By doing the activities in this section you will be helping children to:

- think about the ways in which one event can lead to others
- identify some of their own trigger events and feelings
- think about how their thoughts and behaviours might affect their interactions with other people.

25. Just because

Wellbeing focus:

☑ Self-awareness   ☑ Self and others

Examples of personal skills learned or consolidated:

☑ Taking turns   ☑ Understanding cause and effect
☑ Sequencing

Example of general/social learning:

☑ Exploring links between
   thoughts, feelings and actions

This game introduces the idea of cause and effect (a theme that is also explored in '26. Consequences'), how feeling angry can affect us physically and how this might affect group interactions.

How to play

Player One describes a very simple event, such as 'I opened the window'. Player Two gives a reason: 'Because I was hot'. Player Three gives a possible conse-quence: 'A bird flew into the house' or 'I sang in the school concert', 'Because the soloist had a sore throat', 'I was spotted by a talent scout'. The next player starts with a new event. Players are encouraged to give the causes and effects as quickly as possible and can be challenged by other players if their answers are not thought to be relevant.

Talk about

Sometimes the outcome of a situation can be very predictable and sometimes it might be unexpected. For example, what might be the consequences of breaking something in anger? What could happen if someone is angry because they have been bullied or teased? What will happen if two children have a fight at school? What might happen if you walk away from a possible conflict situation?

Have you ever been in a difficult situation that turned out to be useful for you?

EXPANSION ACTIVITY 25.1. THE STORIES WE TELL (2)

Help the children to make a list of difficult or uncomfortable feelings (for example, jealousy, frustration, being fed up, feeling angry). Imagine each feeling as a different character in a play or a novel. Make up a story together about all these characters trying to build a cinema or a football stadium. What would happen?

The children then think of some possible opposites for each of these feelings. Make up a story together about another set of builders with these character names. What happens when they are asked to build a hospital or a playground?

These stories are a fun way to explore some of the possible consequences of experiencing uncomfortable emotions for a prolonged period of time. Remind the children that none of the feelings are 'wrong' and also that they can have some control over their feelings.

26. Consequences

Wellbeing focus:

☑ Self-awareness   ☑ Self and others

Examples of personal skills learned or consolidated:

☑ Taking turns   ☑ Understanding cause and effect
☑ Sequencing

Examples of general/social learning:

☑ Developing trust   ☑ Exploring links between
☑ Dramatic awareness   thoughts, feelings and actions

A familiar party game, adapted to give an emphasis to exploring how feeling angry might affect us physically.

How to play

Play the drawing version of this game where each player adds a different part of a body with the aim of drawing 'an angry person'. The first person draws the head and neck and folds down the paper to leave just the bottom of the neck showing for the next person to add the top part of the body, ending at the elbows and waist and so on.

Talk about

Sometimes anger can be dissolved by humour. When might this be appropriate? When would it not be appropriate? Have you ever felt angry about something hat you could laugh about later? Can you think of a time when something unexpected or funny happened because someone was angry?

Note: If you know that a child will respond well to humour, this can sometimes defuse a difficult situation very well. However, it is important that the child's feeling of anger and the trigger for their anger is acknowledged first.

EXPANSION ACTIVITY 26.1. WHAT HAPPENS?

(This activity connects with '27. Living links'.) Complete activity sheet 26.1 together. Draw or write about the link between a thought, a feeling and an action.

Talk about

Sometimes our feelings and thoughts get mixed up. I might feel embarrassed or sad about something, but my body might react as if I am in a scary situation. Then the tension I feel can turn into anger. Sometimes when one person is angry and wants to argue or fight, this causes another person to be angry too, even when they weren't angry before. These are examples of 'triggers' for anger – a situation triggers an angry response. Can you think of some of your triggers for anger? What are some of your triggers for happy feelings?

27. Living links

Wellbeing focus:

☑ Self-awareness ☑ Self and others

Examples of personal skills learned or consolidated:

☑ Taking turns ☑ Understanding cause and effect

Examples of general/social learning:

☑ Developing trust
☑ Exploring links between thoughts, feelings and actions

☑ Dramatic awareness
☑ Appreciating similarities and differences

How to play

Players stand in a circle. The game coordinator chooses someone to start off a 'living link'. This person calls out something that makes them feel angry. Anyone who feels angry for the same reason holds hands with the first person and then calls out a different trigger to their anger. When several players respond at the same time, it is the last person in the chain who calls out the next link. This continues until all players are connected. If the whole group connects after only two or three triggers have been named, players can break and re-group, starting with a new caller.

While players are still holding hands, they talk briefly about anger as a chain reaction, triggered by an event and a thought.

Invite the children to dissolve the anger chain by slowly letting go of each other's hands. Get everyone to shake their arms, hands, shoulders and legs.

Adaptations

- Players stay seated in the circle and use string to connect to each other instead of holding hands.
- The game coordinator calls out possible triggers in quick succession and everyone has to group and re-group as fast as they can.

- The game coordinator calls out links for 'excitement' or 'boredom' or 'motivation'.

Talk about

Talk about the similarities and differences in triggers to anger. What happens if someone is angry for several different reasons? Talk about the strength of the anger chain. When might this be a very positive aspect of anger? When might it lead to difficulties?

28. Sorted!

Wellbeing focus:

☑ Self-awareness   ☑ Self and others

Examples of personal skills learned or consolidated:

☑ Observation   ☑ Problem-solving
☑ Listening   ☑ Cooperation
☑ Organizing

Examples of general/social learning:

☑ Being part of a group   ☑ Understanding that events and consequences consist of a series of thoughts, feelings and actions

(This links with '3. Sort us out'.)

How to play

The group is divided into teams. Each team is given a prepared set of cards describing a sequence of events that lead to the successful use of self-calming strategies. There should be enough stages for each child to have one card. The children are timed as they sort themselves into a line to show the correct order.

For example:

- You tell your brother not to borrow your clothes without asking.
- You count to 10.
- You think your younger brother has taken it.
- You congratulate yourself.
- You notice that your jaw is tight and your fists are clenched.
- You can't find your favourite t-shirt.
- You go and find your brother.
- You take two full breaths and relax your hands.

Adaptations

- For smaller groups, pairs of children decide which order the cards should go in and then lay them on the floor for other pairs to see.
- The children stand on a PE bench and then try to arrange themselves without stepping off the bench.
- Groups of children collaborate to decide their own sequence of events. This time they start from the end point of a situation (success in self-calming, for instance) and work backwards to the trigger point. For example:

8. I feel calmer and more in control.

7. I take five minutes out in my quiet space.

6. I remove myself from the situation.

5. I relax my hands and shoulders.

4. I take two full breaths.

3. I notice that my hands and jaw are clenched.

2. I am angry.

1. I am embarrassed.

By working through a self-calming strategy in this way, children are forming a future memory 'as if' the event had already happened. This can be more powerful than planning what to do.

Notice and congratulate strategies well remembered. Finish the activity with a few minutes of relaxation and calm breathing for all the children.

Complete a Goal Record sheet (activity sheet 28.1).

29. Pass the message

Wellbeing focus:

- ☑ Self-awareness
- ☑ Self and others

Examples of personal skills learned or consolidated:

- ☑ Focusing attention
- ☑ Memory strategies

- ☑ Taking turns
- ☑ Tolerating frustration

Examples of general/social learning:

- ☑ Understanding different perspectives
- ☑ Developing self-respect and respect for others

This well-known 'Whispers' game is a fun way of demonstrating how what we say can be misinterpreted or distorted. It also promotes tolerance of mild frustration. The next activity, '30. Cartoons', expands this theme to touch on bias and stereotyping.

How to play

Players are seated in a circle. Player One whispers a short sentence to the next person in the circle, who whispers it to the next person and so on, until it gets back to Player One again. The final sentence heard is then compared to the original version.

Adaptations

- Player One draws a simple shape or picture with one finger on the back of Player Two, who has to pass it on around the circle.
- Player One draws a simple picture on a piece of paper, then shows it briefly to Player Two who has to draw it from memory before showing the new version to Player Three, and so on.

Talk about

How can facts be distorted and how can rumours be spread? Compare the different versions of the pictures or the spoken sentences. Is it easy or difficult to remember the details of what we see and hear? How can things we say and do be remembered inaccurately? What should we do if we think someone is spreading false rumours about us or has been given wrong information about us?

30. Cartoons

Wellbeing focus:

☑ Self-awareness   ☑ Self and others

Examples of personal skills learned or consolidated:

☑ Cooperation   ☑ Understanding stereotypes
☑ Observation   ☑ Sequencing/story-telling
☑ Taking turns

Examples of general/social learning:

☑ Developing self-respect and   ☑ Developing sensitivity to
   respect for others   other people's strengths and
                                           differences

(See also '29. Pass the message'.)

How to play
Players divide into small groups. Each group collaborates to make a cartoon or a collage of a scene depicting some sort of conflict or a situation where at least one person is feeling angry. Groups then share their cartoons and try to guess what each other's pictures represent.

Adaptation

- Players divide into small groups and devise a one-minute silent play, depicting a scene of conflict or a situation where at least one person is angry. They then act out their plays for the rest of the group to guess the situation.

Talk about
Can these plays and pictures be interpreted in different ways? Was there any indication of bias or stereotyping? How are these relevant to feelings of anger and to managing angry feelings?

VII

Recognizing Achievements and Celebrating

These activities provide an opportunity for recapping and celebrating. You might also give time for children to vote for a favourite game to play – just for fun!

31. Finger puppets

Each child uses their own unique fingerprint(s) as a starting point for a drawing or painting of a person.

How to play

Players cut out their own figures and make up a short puppet show in which the figures tell something about themselves to the rest of the group. This does not necessarily have to be directly linked to anger.

Adaptations

- The children make up puppet shows depicting a variety of situations where frustration, annoyance or anger might be displayed. These feelings could be resolved or unresolved by the end of the performance. The group could then contribute ideas for what the puppets could do next.
- Introduce a thumb print puppet as an arbitrator or friend.
- Use shadow puppets instead of fingerprint puppets.

Talk about

Discuss the uniqueness of fingerprints and how each of us is a unique person in some way.

What skills did the 'arbitrator' puppet use? (Give praise for strategies that are well remembered.)

32. Emblems of success

(See also 'Expansion activity 2.1. Superpower shield'.)

How to play

Players each draw the shape of a shield on a large piece of paper. They divide the shield into four sections and draw different symbols or pictures in each section to show successful strategies that they have used for coping with angry feelings.

Some possible new strategies that they may now be using are:

- talking with a friend
- asking for help to solve the difficulty
- listening to some relaxing music
- respecting and valuing oneself
- respecting and valuing other people
- walking away from conflict situations
- finding a quiet space to 'chill out'.

Display the shields on a table or wall. Players guess the owner of each one.

Adaptations

- The children draw a shield for 'My hopes for next year' or 'My motto'.
- Make one large coat of arms for the whole group.

Talk about

What are the similarities and differences between the shields? (Celebrate times when the children have used their strategies successfully.)

33. Variety show

Players will need to have plenty of preparation time before this game.

How to play
Invite the children (as volunteers) to take turns in showing the rest of the group something that creatively expresses how they manage strong emotions. This could be an object chosen from home (such as a photograph, a book or a favourite toy), a short piece of music (drum beats or a well-known song), a drawing, a dance, a single movement, a short story, a poem – absolutely anything at all! No interpretation is needed unless the children want to explain the relevance of what they have chosen. The children each give their presentation and the group respond with applause and praise.

Adaptation

- Players choose something they are wearing or something they have with them on the day (so no need for any preparation), and say in what way it reflects their own personality, and then how this aspect of their personality is going to help them in managing their angry feelings.

34. Pass the shell

How to play

Use a large shell or a beautiful or unusual object of some sort. Pass the object around the group. Whoever is holding it praises someone else and passes them the object. This is best done in sequence around the circle, unless you feel that children can praise each other in random order and not leave anyone out.

Adaptations

- Each child has a piece of paper and writes their name at the bottom. The pieces of paper are passed around the group for everyone to write something positive about the person named on the paper. The paper is folded over after each comment has been added so that no one sees what anyone else has written. The paper is then returned to the original player to read when they want to.
- Everyone has a piece of paper pinned to their back for others to write their praise on.
- The children write a letter to themselves with advice and praise for how well they have done. This letter can be posted to them or handed to them at an agreed time in the future (two weeks is usually helpful) as a reminder and a boost to their confidence.

35. Winning the Oscars

How to play

Cover a wooden spoon or an artist's figure with tin foil. Present this to each child in turn at an imaginary 'award ceremony' for whatever they would most like to have an award for. This could be a past achievement, a future goal or something completely fantastical. Really over-play their achievement. The whole group celebrates each award with plenty of clapping and cheering, etc.

Adaptations

- Players take turns to be a 'national treasure'. The rest of the group take turns to walk up to this person and shake their hands or give words of praise or thanks.
- And finally – have your own celebration as well!

VIII

Activity Sheets

The activity sheets in this section can be adapted for discussion or used as a basis for devising more complex activity sheets for older children.

Where possible, I suggest that you encourage children to draw rather than to write, and to work together rather than to sit quietly completing activity sheets on their own. This sharing and talking will not only help to foster collaborative, mutually respectful relationships, it also offers an opportunity for each child to enrich their understanding of the benefits of using imagery, being mindful and thinking creatively.

ACTIVITY SHEET 4.1. SKILLS WHEEL

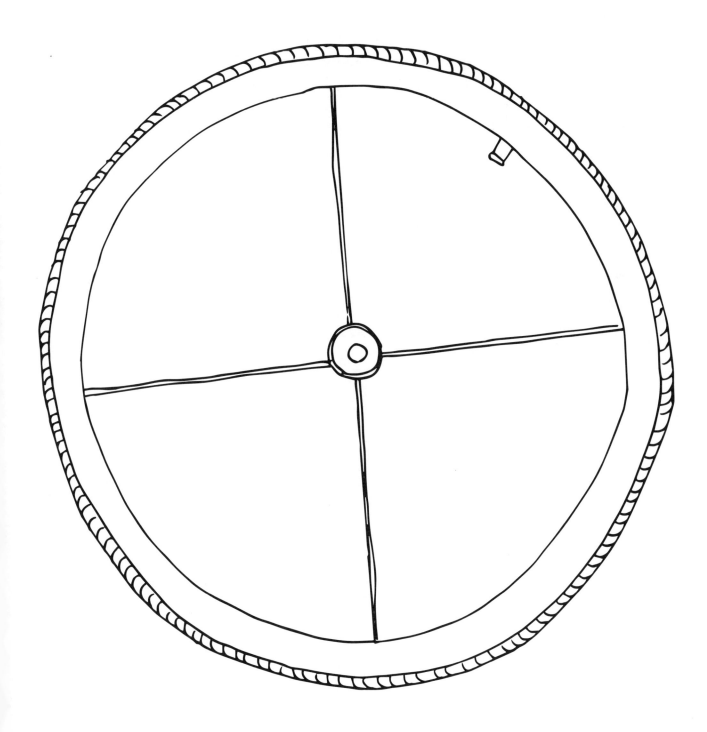

ACTIVITY SHEET 4.2. PRAISE

When someone has done something well or really tried hard with something, they might be praised for it. The good thing about praise is that it can happen at any time and for *lots* of different reasons. We can praise other people and we can praise ourselves too.

To praise someone means

....

....

....

....

I can praise people by

....

....

....

....

When people praise me I feel

....

....

....

....

Today I praised someone for

....

....

....

....

Something I would like to be praised for is

....

....

....

....

Today I praised myself for

....

....

....

....

ACTIVITY SHEET 8.1. IMAGINING

Let's check out what your imagination is like today. Ask someone to read 'Think of a chocolate cake' to you. While you are listening, imagine that you can see, hear, feel, taste and smell all the things that the person tells you about.

Think of a chocolate cake

Sit comfortably and close your eyes. Imagine that you are at home in the kitchen. Imagine that it is your birthday, and someone has made you a huge great chocolate cake. It is in the fridge. You are allowed to go and get it.

Imagine yourself opening the fridge door. You see the cake on a big plate. What does it look like? You take it out of the fridge. What does the plate feel like? How do you carry the cake? What can you smell? You put the plate with the cake on it onto a table. Someone comes and cuts a big slice for you. What does this person say while they are cutting the cake?

What happens to the cake as this person starts to cut it? You reach out to take the piece of cake. What does it feel like when you touch it? Then you take a big bite. What can you taste? Can you smell anything? What do you imagine yourself saying? Now let the images fade and, when you're ready, open your eyes.

Now you are giving your imagination a good work out!

ACTIVITY SHEET 19.1. LOOK OUT FOR ICEBERGS

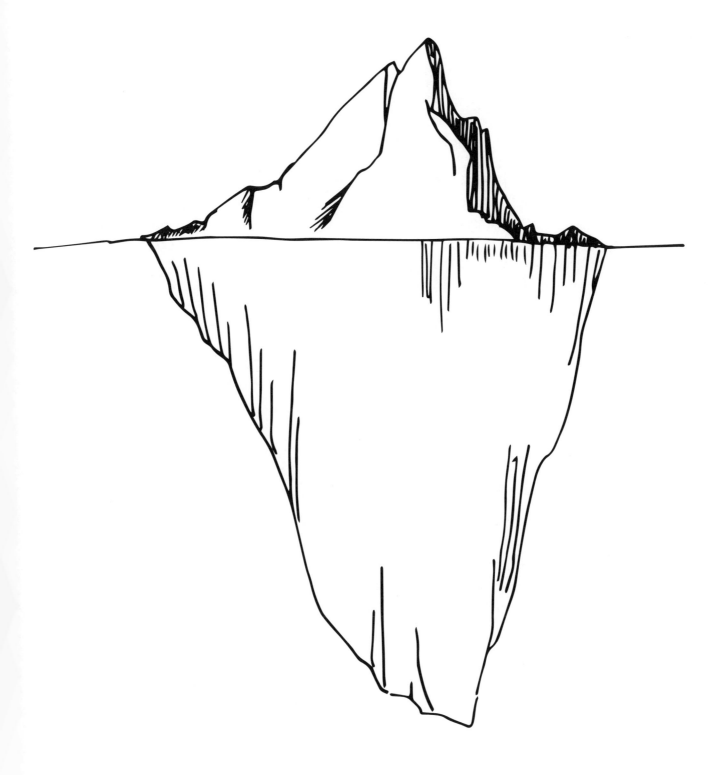

ACTIVITY SHEET 22.1. I CAN CHANGE THE WAY I FEEL

When I am feeling _____ this is what I can do:

☐

☐

☐

☐

☐

☐

ACTIVITY SHEET 22.2. TROUBLESOME TIGERS

Think of all the things that you could do when an angry thought starts to growl at you.

....

....

....

....

....

....

....

....

....

ACTIVITY SHEET 23.2. WHAT DOES ANGER FEEL LIKE?

Have you ever got angry about something that hasn't happened yet?
What did your body feel like?

....

....

....

....

....

....

....

....

Can you think of any other feelings that you might get when you are angry?

....

....

....

....

....

....

....

....

....

Have you ever got excited about something long before it happened? What did your body feel like then?

....

....

....

....

....

....

....

....

....

....

Your imagination can make your body feel different things. Sometimes this is good, but sometimes this is not useful for you.

Sometimes you can change what you are imagining so that you can *feel* better.

Imagine that!

ACTIVITY SHEET 26.1. WHAT HAPPENS?

I think this:

I feel this:

I do this:

Then this happens:

ACTIVITY SHEET 28.1. SORTED!

My Goal Record sheet

My goal is:

....

....

....

I tried it when:

....

....

....

This is what happened:

....

....

....

The next thing I'm going to try is:

....

....